THROUGH ADOPTED HEARTS

A COLLECTION OF MEMOIRS FROM
BIRTH AND ADOPTIVE PARENTS

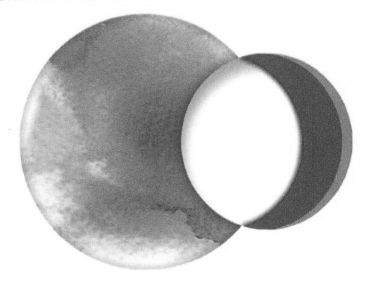

WRITTEN & COMPILED BY
ELENA S HALL

[Word.robe] Media

2020

First Edition, February 2020

ISBN: 978-0-578-61919-4

1. Nonfiction - Family & Relationships   2. Nonfiction - Adoption & Fostering 3. Nonfiction - Biography, Personal Memoirs

Published by Wordrobe Media
Printed and distributed through Kindle Direct Publishing.

Cover design by Liz Housewright

Editing and layout by Jonathan Jordan

www.wordrobemedia.com

PRAISE FOR ELENA S. HALL'S FIRST BOOK,
THROUGH ADOPTED EYES

"A testimony to the depth of need and pain we bring to the table as sojourners in this world, along with the depth of hope that is possible for, in, and through those on the adoption and permanency spectrum.

-Cameron Lee Small, MS, LPCC, *Therapy Redeemed*

"It is humbling to be offered a window into each of these stories. The entries are encouraging and simultaneously refuse to paint a simple picture of adoption…All these voices together give you the broadest understanding of ALL the complexities of adoption."

-Lanaya Graham, *Adoption Books*

To The Triad

CONTENTS

ACKNOWLEDGEMENTS i

FOREWORD iii

INTRODUCTION 1

PART ONE: THE BIRTH PARENTS

ABBIE	25
APRIL	32
AUBREY	38
BROOKLYN	44
CAMILA	46
DESIRAE	49
ERICA	54
KELSEY	58
LINDIE	64
MONIQUA	66
NORA	70
REAGAN	73
SAMANTHA	75

SARAH   81
SKYLAR   86
TIA   90

PART TWO: THE ADOPTIVE PARENTS

ALLISON   99
AMELIA   102
BETHANY   119
CHARLOTTE & MASON   122
CHRISTA   127
DANIELLE & FORD   137
ELIZABETH   142
JENNIFER   147
KALEB & DEMI   151
KENDALL   155
LEIGHA   159
LENA   165
LILI   171
LORI   178
MADELINE   180
MICHELE   191
PENNY   200
SHANNON   206

BUILDING HEARTS

215

STORY INDEX

219

RECOMMENDED RESOURCES   222

ABOUT THE AUTHOR   225

ACKNOWLEDGEMENTS

Since I began connecting with fellow adoptees and writing down many of my own thoughts about adoption, I have finished graduate school and am now working as a social worker with members of the adoption triad.

After *Through Adopted Eyes* was published, it was so exciting to hear powerful stories from all different people about how the book had impacted them and opened up conversations. But I quickly realized that there needed to be another book, this time to usher readers into the world of both birth and adoptive parents. I emailed Jonathan, my wonderful editor, and we got started right away in Spring of 2019.

If you know, are a member of, or work with someone connected to adoption, I hope that this book promotes healing and comfort, and provides education and a good read for you. Keep sharing stories. Keep writing. There is a lot to learn about how adoption affects people. I learned a lot compiling these stories and working on this book, so I hope you do, too.

To you, the reader, thank you for seeking insight through adopted hearts.

To the birth and adoptive parents featured in this book, thank you for your stories and for sharing a piece of your heart with me.

Let's Connect! I would love to hear from you!

Email: throughadoptedeyesbook@gmail.com
Instagram: @throughadoptedeyes

FOREWORD

By Adrian Collins

Adoption permeates our society. Its impact weaves in and out of our communities. Voices of adoption whisper throughout our schools, our families, and our places of work. There was a time that I never thought I'd become a voice for adoption. It was a foreign concept, a faraway notion - until I was directly impacted by its grasp.

It wasn't until I was faced with my own unexpected pregnancy as a junior in college that adoption took on a personal meaning. I'd dreamed of becoming a mom for as long as I could remember. I longed to wrap my arms around my newborn and rock her to sleep every night. I imagined what it would be like to take her hand in mine and walk her to the park. I thought about what it'd be like to braid her hair. I romanticized motherhood.

Yet, I also understood what it meant to provide emotionally and financially as a parent. I weighed my options carefully and sought counseling at a local adoption agency.

In the end, I would sacrifice my dreams so that my daughter could have hers.

Leaving the hospital without my daughter is the single hardest thing I've ever done. I shed tears of immense grief. At times, the heartache was consuming.

After placing my daughter for adoption, I returned to college afraid that others wouldn't understand my choice. I avoided the incessant whispers by hanging my head in silent shame. I longed for a friend who understood my journey. I was afraid to share my story in fear of rejection from my teachers and peers, so I kept my voice hidden.

I kept silent for years about my decision to place a child for adoption.

Hundreds of seasons would come and go after I'd said goodbye to my daughter. As the years passed, my home filled to the brim with children. I'd married my high school sweetheart and birth father to my daughter, and given birth to three boys.

But I'd yet to find my voice.

One day, I decided to break the chains of silence and start sharing my story. I began by volunteering as a mentor to birth moms to walk alongside them and help them navigate the process of adoption. When I shared my story of being a birth mom, I felt empowered. I found freedom. The layers of shame and guilt began to melt away.

I never imagined that using my voice to mentor others would forever change my family.

One of the birth moms I mentored was a family friend who had encountered an unexpected pregnancy. During one meeting, she turned to me and asked softly, "Will you adopt my baby boy?"

A few months later, she placed her sweet baby boy in my arms and I became an adoptive mom. We brought our son home and showered him with abundant love.

But then questions of doubt began. *Will I love him the same as my other children? Do I have enough love for everyone?*

While I reveled in motherhood, I succumbed to silent fears as an adoptive mom. I rocked my son at bedtime and wondered, "Does anyone share the same doubts as me?" I focused on being the perfect adoptive mom instead of openly sharing my struggles and hardships.

I longed for a community. I wished for a safe place to share my voice, and to hear from others.

According to Adoption Network, "Nearly 100 million Americans have adoption in their immediate family," and "six in ten Americans have had a personal experience with adoption, meaning that they themselves, a family member, or close friend was adopted, had adopted a child, or had placed a child for adoption."

If so, one can assume that nearly 100 million Americans have encountered some form of trauma, joy, grief, healing, heartache, acceptance, fears, bonding, doubts and unconditional love. It also means that over 100 million Americans have a voice to offer insight, perspective, and awareness.

Without a voice, those impacted by adoption remain hidden in our midst. Without a voice, false stigmas, myths and perceptions about adoption run rampant.

This is why I'm thrilled for Elena's latest book, *Through Adopted Hearts* that gives a voice to those in the adoption community. These contributors open our eyes, ears, and minds about the reality of adoption and what we can learn from those inside the Triad.

Community is at the very core of this book. Its pages are filled with messages of hope, awareness, and enduring love. Its contents provide a sense of community for birth mothers, adoptees and adoptive parents. These stories are a road map to acceptance, understanding and belonging. Finally, the book serves as a resource to adoptive families to understand what's at the very core of adoption.

We want you, Birth Parent, Adoptive Parent and Adoptee to know you are not alone. Thank you, Elena, for giving us a safe place to share our stories and shed light on the heart of adoption.

Adrian Collins is a writer, speaker, birth mom, adoptive mom, and advocate for adoption education. You can learn more about her at adrianccollins.com and follow her on Instagram @adrianccollins

INTRODUCTION

WELCOME TO THE TRIAD

Have you ever heard of the adoption triad? Well, for those of you who haven't, it's made up of three key ingredients: adoptees, adoptive parents, and birth parents.

This handy image here represents the adoption triad, with each point of the triangle representing a member mentioned above. Existing within this triad, one discovers it is filled with many intricacies that cause all its members to be impacted by adoption in different ways.

Do you know any members of the adoption triad? Maybe you do and don't even realize it, but there are a lot of us out there whose stories need to be shared. There are also a lot of us out there who haven't figured out how to share our stories yet.

As an adoptee from Russia, it is important for me to share my story and what adoption means to me, and if you already read my first book, *Through Adopted Eyes: A Collection of Memoirs from Adoptees,* then you know many of my thoughts on adoption. Also, it provides a glimpse into the world of fifty adoptees of different backgrounds and perspectives, showing how complex and emotional adoption can be, and how no two adoption stories are the same. And if you haven't read it, then here is my shameless plug for you to get it and read the adoptees' perspectives!

Birth and adoptive parents each have a piece of their heart invested in one another.

The whole goal of *this* book is for adoptive parents and birth parents to have a turn and share their perspectives as the remaining members of the triad. Now, what comes to mind when you think about birth parents and those who make an adoption plan for their birth child? What comes to your mind when I mention people who adopt?

Birth parents and adoptive parents - that topic alone is a lot for an adoptee like me to write about because, well, where do you even start? I guess I will begin by saying that the inspiration for the title of this book came from the fact that birth and adoptive parents each have a piece of their heart invested in one another *and* in the adoptee that binds them together in the triangle of the triad.

While adoption always includes deep feelings and hard decisions, it would not be true to say this depth is experienced the same way for each person or in every situation; there is variety in every story. But adoption - whether making a plan for a child or choosing to bring a child into your family - is a huge life decision, a massive transition that has to be made by both parties. And every transition or life change involves heart. So it is important to view the many shades of adoption through adopted hearts to see how lives are interwoven together in the adoption triad from the viewpoint of the birth and adoptive parents.

The stories in this book are heartfelt and important to help us all understand the parents' part of the story. These two corners of the triad are (usually) the ones that have a decision, a choice, and some sort of power in the adoption decision. Meanwhile, the adoptees usually have no say, no control in the process.

Of course, there are exceptions. Some adoptees, those who are older or from foster care, have some power to make choices in their adoption stories. And yes, some expectant parents were forced or shamed and coerced into making an adoption plan to place their children for adoption, but today many domestic infant adoptions include empowering both the birth *and* adoptive members.

This book, just like the last, was a joy and honor to put together and relied heavily on reaching out through social media. It is not as if I went searching the globe for the most dramatic stories, but I just started by letting people know that I was working on a second book. Then birth and adoptive parents sent me messages expressing interest in sharing their stories and I sent them a list of questions. Everyone sent me their recorded replies to the questions and it's truly incredible how everyone shared their heart with me and trusted me with their story. I don't take that responsibility lightly for a second. I see myself as a steward of these stories, which prove that all adoption journeys are important, powerful, and unique.

I'm not an expert. In fact, I've learned a lot through this process. One thing that surprised me when reading the birth parent stories was how encouraged I felt because it reminded me there is hope behind the personal vagueness and unknowns in my own story! It helped me think about possible things my own birth parents might have thought or experienced before and after I was placed for adoption.

I believe that writing is so important because it pushes the writer to put all of their thoughts, experiences, and being into words. Writing has the power to propel thoughts - good and bad - through the page and into the mind and heart of the reader. The people in this book understand why it is important to share stories. Although it requires vulnerability, it also helps us all to grow more. There is always more to learn about from each other, more stories to share.

TREAD LIGHTLY

It is always interesting what people say about adoption. You never quite know what they are going to say because there are so many misconceptions and downright confusing subjects surrounding adoption. This isn't helped by media betrayal that either oversimplifies adoption by making it fluffy and pretty or by making all adoptions look like a horror movie, perpetuating negative stereotypes through both fiction and nonfiction routes because sensationalism is what sells.

So, when I say adoption conversations are always *interesting,* I mean that comments are unpredictable; some will be positive and some will be negative. I am usually on-edge after I mention something about adoption because I never know how the other person will respond. Like other sensitive topics, everyone has their own ideas about adoption formed through their worldview and experiences.

Sitting at an auto shop waiting to get my car fixed, a typical, dad-type guy started talking about his car troubles. (We'll call him Fred, though I bet that wasn't his real name.) Anyway, Fred and I talked back and forth about what repairs needed to be done to our respective vehicles. While we were chatting, another lady was sitting in a chair next to mine and she was knitting, also waiting for her car to be worked on (we'll call her Ethel for kicks).

Somehow, Fred started talking about his family and his adopted sister. I mentioned that I wanted to work as an adoption professional in some way. Fred then mentioned that his parents had to wait six years to adopt his sister.

Then I hear: "Do you know what would solve that adoption waiting problem?"

This question was from Ethel, who I assume had heard the entirety of our conversation.

I stared at her, eager for her to share her amazing plan to solve waiting for adoptive placement.

"Dogs!" she exclaimed proudly.

Yes... Yes, you read that right. She said *dogs*. Like, the animal. *Bark bark*...

So naturally, I just stared at her, speechless. Would there be any good reply to this? Both Fred and I just stared, unable to think of what to say.

So, Ethel the knitting dog lady continued on:

"Yes, my children are my dogs and we did not have to wait years to adopt them!"

I told her that her dogs sounded great and Fred started talking about all of his Rottweilers.

It was *ruff.* (Sorry, I couldn't resist.)

There is still so much that we can all learn - my adopted self included - about adoption (of humans). But this lady did not think about what her words might mean to someone else. I doubt she evaluated how parents would feel discussing adoption and then having it be compared to her dogs.

Maybe this is a good time to mention that I actually love dogs and see nothing wrong with adopting dogs, but the fact that the word *adoption* can be applied to both scenarios is another topic entirely. While I suppose there can be similarities in the different types of adoptions, it is absurd to compare human adoptions to the adoption of animals. In my opinion, I think we should *rescue* animals and save the term *adoption* for humans.

When people use the word adoption in any other context outside of the adoption of a human, it could be interpreted as an insult because it glosses over the depth of the adoption process. It makes light of the subject, which is not a light subject at all. So I really hate when people say "adopt a highway" or "adopt a soldier for the holidays." Have you seen these signs?

Instead, maybe we should say "sponsor a highway" and "support a soldier." And it is also frustrating when people caption photos that say something like, "this is my adopted sister" synonymously with "best friend." Or if someone goes out of town and stays with friends and the hosts say they *adopted* that guest for the weekend...

No, no you didn't.

I know it may sound to some like I am getting overly-sensitive, but it is important to know that the word *adoption* carries a lot of weight and meaning to the adoption triad. We cannot just allow the word adoption be thrown around and used to describe a mix of things because it ends up compromising the true significance of the word.

Terminology is important and the misuse of adoption language is one reason why explaining adoption is already so difficult. I am proud to call myself an adoptee, but if everyone says they want to adopt a friend for the weekend or someone wishes so-and-so was their adoptive sibling, it cheapens the word *adoption* and takes away from those who truly are living lives directly impacted by adoption, aka, the adoption triad.

FAIRYTALE IDEAS

When I was younger, I had a fairytale notion of adoption, where my adoptive parents were perfect and it was just a happy life. But as I got older, I realized nothing is as perfect as it seems and there was a big piece of myself that was absent from my present reality, and that was really disheartening. I guess this fairytale faded as I grew up and gained understanding that adoption involves both gains *and* losses. It's not that I felt incomplete exactly, but the realization that I lost something made my fairytale feel less perfect.

While I care greatly for my birth parents, I just do not know why they relinquished their rights and made me adoptable. It is hard for me not to

In the end, no parent is perfect. No child is perfect. No process is perfect..

envy other adoptees I meet, because they usually have more information on their birth family than I do. Information may even be known about the circumstances surrounding their adoption and some adoptees may even have visits with birth families. But I am also thankful for the information that I do know and the experiences that I have.

Of course, not all adoptions are *open adoptions* where there is a line of open communication between an adoptee's birth family and adoptive family, but many fellow adoptees I meet have some kind of contact or information. This contact seems to be a wonderful thing when appropriate and respected by both parties.

There are many kinds of adoptions: embryo, international, domestic, and adoption after foster care. Likewise, there are many reasons children are adopted, many reasons birth parents make an adoption plan, and many reasons adoptive parents decide to adopt. In the end, no parent is perfect. No child is perfect. No process is perfect.

I think it can be really easy for a member of the adoption triad to generalize other members of the triad. For example, an adoptive parent may automatically assign a trait to every other adoptive parent, birth parent, and adoptee based solely on the people that make up their specific adoption triad. People tend to project their expectations onto others based solely on their personal experience. It would be like me assuming that, just because I have great adoptive parents, then all adoptive parents must be equally great! But, as you may have learned in my first book, that is not always the case.

I wish everyone could have a positive outlook on adoption like me, but that dream is not realistic. But it's also not fair to assume your life experience gets to define everyone else's experience. That is why it is good to hear from varying perspectives. Not all birth parents are the same. Not all adoptive parents are the same.

Again, there is not really a mold for these kinds of things. There is not a cookie-cutter definition of any type of triad member that fits into a perfect world in a little fairytale dream house. Adoptive or not, there is no perfect family. But that does not mean that families cannot mold and create their own dream house, just so long as they acknowledge how that fairytale came together. After all, fairytales are not always just happiness and rainbows - they involve ups and downs, trials and conflict that the characters have to overcome.

The issue is, I used to only zoom in to the happy sections of my personal fairytale. I liked the happy tunes playing while everyone lives happily ever after, but that only happened because the dragon had to be defeated first! Likewise, it's easy to zoom in on the negative things and neglect the positive chapters of the story.

But if we can all zoom out and see how the story came together - ups and downs, trials and conflict - then we can truly get an appreciation for each of our own stories in the broader context of our shared experiences. We can zoom out to see how the good points in our story came to pass. We can be thankful for each character who has played a role in each of our stories thus far. Whether you are in the midst of a trial or in a time of peace right now, I hope you can zoom out and find thankfulness for how it all fits together.

A QUARTER FOR YOUR THOUGHTS

I had my suitcase all packed, including a giant seven-pound bag of fruity candy to make my book booth more appealing. I had printed business cards and bookmarks, too. Suddenly, I realized how books really make suitcases a lot heavier… So there I was, huffing and puffing as I rolled my bag to the gate at the airport waiting to go to another adoption conference and connect with all members of the triad that might be there. I sat down, catching my breath after lugging this luggage across the airport.

"So, what do you have in there that is so heavy?" said a kind lady in a bright blue cardigan.

I told her I was going to a conference with my books, where I would get to share about adoption. We started talking about her life and how she was excited about visiting her family and shared with me that her daughter was adopted! We were laughing and having a grand old time, and then I looked up and saw an elderly gentleman extending a quarter to me and my new blue cardigan buddy.

Holding out the quarter, the elderly gentleman said, "I just wanted to give you both a small award for bringing joy to this gate!"

It really made my whole day! I kept the quarter in my pocket to remind myself of how important it is to spread joy each and every day...even at the airport.

After I arrived at the conference, I got to meet a lot of people, including other members of the triad, which was both a very exciting and healing thing for me. I did not realize how much I was subconsciously ascribing both good and bad characteristics to fellow adoptees, birth parents, and adoptive parents based on myself, my birth parents, and my adoptive parents.

At the conference, I got to talk to a group of ladies about how adoptees are the only member in the triad who were assigned to their triad

Birth and adoptive parents have years of events leading up to when the adoptee enters into the story,

position. Pregnancy is just the beginning of the journey for adoptive parents and birth parents alike. Birth parents and adoptive parents get to process whether they *want* to be involved in the world of adoption - it's a choice for them. Meanwhile, the adoptees almost always have that decision made *for* them. Birth and adoptive parents have years of events leading up to when the adoptee enters into the story, so it is important to find out more about the inner workings of what makes up two-thirds of the triad.

Hearing from birth mothers at the conference and having real life-giving conversations with these ladies was important to me because I have not (and probably never will) have a chance to have a conversation with my birth parents, since my personal story is that of a closed international adoption. Birth parents today sometimes have some kind of control over the level of openness they have with their bio child.

Thankfully, some of the old-fashioned stereotypes that made adoption a "hush hush" topic have fallen to the wayside. To me, being able to encourage birth parents by telling them that their ability to tell their birth children the "why" behind their adoption journeys is such a blessing. I got to tell birth parents that they have a special opportunity to tell their bio children stories about their lives and experiences.

I would love to know the "why" behind my adoption and something about my birth parents. Today, birth parents in open adoptions can gift these stories to their bio-children and the adoptive parents in a way that many closed adoptions cannot.

At the conference, adoptive parents expressed joy and empathy with other triad members, as well as stories of being parents. It was so humbling to see hopeful adoptive parents come and learn - and I was learning with them. Many expressed that rather than saying adoptive parents "save" their child, one should instead refer to it as a commitment they are making to be that child's loving and supportive parent. Some hated the term "Gotcha Day" while other adoptive parents loved it. Many hopeful adoptive parents were still in the pre-triad phase of waiting for a match with a birth family or placement with a new child.

It was also interesting to discuss how each triad member is judged. For example, one person may have negative feelings about the birth parents in their specific triad and then disgrace or judge *all* birth parents on

Adoption turns strangers into families.

social media. One adoptive parent told me she had hateful comments online from someone claiming her child should not even be in their family.

As an adoptee myself, I have never received such comments but instead receive more pity comments or people telling me how loved I should feel solely based on the fact I was chosen. Each of us shared the good messages we had received too, but it was really interesting to see how the stereotypes again played into personal comments on social media.

Because all adoptions are so unique, it is imperative for everyone to constantly come to the table with open arms and open minds. I know that may seem a bit of a stretch to hope for in this day and age, but one can dream, right? And it's possible when we can all just take a deep breath and *listen* to each other - no matter if someone has a positive or negative view of adoption, *listening* is important.

All adoptees are different, and all adoptive and birth parents are also unique. Adoption is powerful because it incites emotions and forever alters the course of those whose lives are involved in it. It turns strangers into families - and in some case, families into strangers. But my hope is that adoption will connect more than it divides.

BOOK TWO

The adoption conversation cannot and should not end at adoptees, however, because then you only have one-third of the triad. With my first book, I wanted to give voice to adoptees, because so often we feel voiceless. But with this book, I wanted people to better understand what the rest of the adoption triad has to say. Let's get the *whole* picture.

Just like my first book, I once again took to social media to share my idea to help tell the rest of the triad's story. This process was very nerve-wracking because it is a big responsibility to try to honor the parts of the triad that I am not a part of. I do not know what it is like to be a birth parent *or* an adoptive parent, so these stories really taught me a lot. Compared to the first book, I found this one very challenging.

Adoptees are accustomed to *not* knowing things, so it's really interesting to talk to the two other points of the triad - to members who together can fill in the pieces of the adoption journey. I got to see how adoption is an emotional journey for everyone involved. It is not only the adoptee that carries weight about the unknown, but birth and adoptive parents, too. That's a common theme for all points of the triad - the unknown.

There are similar struggles and emotions for everyone involved in adoption - and together each member of the adoption triad shares what adoption is like through their eyes, helping to unlock the intricacies of adoption. Again, no story is the same, but that's part of the beauty of it.

The birth parents who participated in sharing their stories received the following questions:

- Tell me about yourself.
- Was the adoption open or closed?
- What does adoption mean to you?
- Why did you make an adoption plan?
- What is the best and worst thing someone has said to you about adoption?

- What do you want others to know about your birth parent experience?
- How did your age at delivery affect your decision to make an adoption plan?
- What are the biggest misconceptions about birth parents?
- Any terms or phrases that you hate? Any phrases you love?
- What do you wish people could understand about your story?
- What is the best part of your adoption story?
- What would you say to adoptees and adoptive parents?

You may not agree with every story or thought – and that's okay – but all of these stories are important.

Likewise, the adoptive parents received the following questions:

- Tell me about yourself.
- What kind of adoption did you all go through? Domestic, Foster-to-Adopt, Embryo? Open or closed?
- Why did you choose adoption?

- How did you approach telling your child their adoption story?
- How old were your children when they found out they were adopted? Would you have changed something about that experience?
- What does adoption mean to you?
- What is the best and worst thing someone has said to you about adoption?
- What do you want others to know about your adoptive parent experience?
- How did your child's age at adoption finalization impact you?
- Did you have a relationship with any of your child's birth relatives? What has that experience been like?
- What do you wish people could understand about your story?
- What is the best part of your adoption story?
- Are their questions you always get asked?
- Any terms or phrases that you hate? Any phrases you love?
- What would you say to adoptees and birth parents?

Not every participant answered every question. Also, slight changes have been made in the editing process to turn these answers into a story. This sometimes meant re-arranging things or updating language, but there were no changes made to their stories, their tone, or their perspectives. No one was told to push a certain agenda and everyone was just told to write their replies and their stories. Rather, these questions were chosen to help prompt them to share their authentic experiences and we wanted to retain that authenticity as much as possible. So take each story for what it is and respect everyone's voice - while also looking at the greater themes that you might discover.

Also, please know that most of the stories included here use pseudonyms for confidentiality, but their words are still their own. I have noted where individuals requested to use their real names.

This conversation gets *real*, really quick, so know that some of this may be hard to digest. You may need to push the "pause" button and take a deep breath. After all, you may not agree with every story or thought - and that's okay - but all of these stories are important. Everyone also had things to rejoice over, too - it's not all gloom and hardship. You will read true stories of adoptive parents and birth parents who fully gave their hearts to this project. There is so much insight, wisdom, and heartfelt sentiment within these pages.

Right now, I want you to clear your head of any kind of stereotypes and generalizations you have about adoption, adoptive parents, and birth parents. Maybe you have your own experiences, maybe you have heard things, or maybe you've just never thought much about it at all. I just want everyone to dispel any previous notions and be open to the forthcoming perspectives. So here is a look at the parents' side of things, stories filtered through adopted hearts.

PART ONE:
THE BIRTH PARENTS

ABBIE

I am a birth mother of almost four years, but that is not all that I am. My story does not begin or end with my pregnancy and placement. I am a lot of things.

I am a survivor of childhood sexual abuse. I struggle with depression and complex PTSD. I got pregnant at seventeen and I chose adoption. But I am so much more than what I've been through.

I am a writer and spend much of my time telling my story, using my words to help others who are grieving. I am a student, finishing up a degree in psychology and headed toward a career in social work.

I am a wife; I have built an amazing healthy relationship with a good man. I will be a mother again someday. I am resilient and proud of the life I have created for myself.

I made an adoption plan because it was the only way to keep my baby safe. The relationship I had with the biological father was abusive - emotionally, physically and mentally. He was also in his mid-twenties and I was a minor. He used our unborn child as a pawn to try and coerce me into marrying him as soon as I turned eighteen. When he realized that wouldn't work, he told me he would fight me for custody just to make sure I never saw her again - not because he wanted to be a father. I wanted my child to grow up with a daddy who she could trust, who would always be there to love and protect her.

My age is part of the reason I placed. I was very young and didn't have the education I needed to get a good job to support us. But more than that, I was immature - just a child myself. Now, just four years later, I have changed so much. I know who I am and what I want. I have learned how to have healthy relationships and set boundaries. I love and respect myself. I didn't have any of these skills when I was eighteen, and it would not have been fair to my sweet babe for her to have to suffer the consequences of my immaturity and the poor choices I was making at the time. I was just a little girl who needed time to grow up.

Choosing adoption didn't mean I wasn't a mother anymore, just a different kind. It means that I am no less than other mothers, and my choice doesn't mean that I'm not perfectly capable of parenting children in the future. It was my *circumstances*, not who I am as a person, that made adoption right for me and my baby at that time.

The adoption is open, so we share text messages and photo updates, follow each other on social media, and have in-person visits about every other month. As long as I am around and available for my birth daughter when she needs me, as long as I let her know my love for her, then I have done the best I could, like all good moms do.

Some people tell me that it's great to see how well I've moved on from that chapter in my life. I want people to know that I am moving forward, but I will never, ever "move on." But since placement, I've made a lot of great changes. I have a good job, a wonderful husband, and I'm finishing up my bachelor's degree. I love my life, but that doesn't mean I've "moved on."

My adoption story isn't over - it is a permanent part of my life even as I am moving forward. The grief cycle will continue in waves throughout my life, and I'm okay with that. I would never want to just forget about my birth daughter - I love her so much and she brings me so much joy.

I truly know the meaning of bittersweet. This experience has an influence on everything I do. I live my life in a way that I hope will make my birth daughter proud. I think of her daily, and I will never be the same...in a good way.

There's a big misconception that all birth mothers are drug addicts who don't care about their unborn child. I have had a lot of struggles in my life, but addiction is not one of them. Substance abuse has never been an issue for me. In fact, during my pregnancy, I exercised and ate well. I never missed a doctor's appointment or prenatal vitamin. I loved the child I was carrying with all my heart and I would never have done anything to put her in jeopardy.

Another misconception is that women who choose adoption are looking to gain financial support in exchange for their child. I certainly did not place my child to try and make money. I paid a hundred percent of my living expenses during and after my pregnancy. Paying my bills wasn't always easy, but I didn't take a dime from my baby's new parents. My child was *not* for sale.

Another misconception is that if a birth mother isn't a drug addict, then she is a thoughtless teenager who sleeps around and doesn't think about protection, choosing adoption as a way to get out of the responsibilities of motherhood. There are many reasons that a woman might get pregnant: lack of access to birth control, a broken condom, an assault, etcetera.

Someone told me that I should not have been included in a church activity with other girls my age. That since I was pregnant, I wasn't a good example to them and that choosing adoption was a way of "getting away with it." The implication that I was just abandoning my child because I didn't want the responsibility was so hurtful, and honestly it's hard for me to think about today. I am not a bad example! I had been through a lot and was doing the best I could for my baby.

So please don't make judgements about the decision-making skills of a woman simply because she became pregnant unexpectedly. And yes, I was a teenager but that didn't mean I was running from responsibility by choosing to place for adoption. I didn't place because I cared more about going to parties; I placed because I knew I was not in the position to give my child the life she deserved.

I wish people knew how much I love my child! Many people can't wrap their heads around why I would **Adoption makes a family tree become an orchard.** choose adoption if I truly loved my baby. Wouldn't I want to keep her with me? Wouldn't I sacrifice everything for her? Of course, I wanted to parent. I wanted to rock her to sleep, to be there for her first day of kindergarten, to be the one to comfort her when she gets her heart broken for the first time.

But it wasn't about my wants. It was about the life I could realistically give her. I had to face facts, and that meant that it was likely she would have a childhood torn between her father and I, no stability, no money, no example of a healthy relationship. I placed because of how much I love her. I know that being adopted can be traumatic. That's valid. But I believe that because I chose adoption, she will be able to learn the tools she needs to deal with that difficulty much better than she would have been able to cope with a childhood exposed to the trials she would have had to endure.

I love the saying that adoption makes a family tree become an orchard. It's so true! Both birth and adoptive families are real and contribute to the child's life in different ways. An orchard can produce so much beautiful fruit, just like the love we all share can nourish our child throughout their life.

It goes without saying that the term "give up" or "give away" is damaging. You give away old furniture to the thrift store, but you do not give away human beings. A related phrase is that a birth mother "gives the gift of adoption" to adoptive parents. Children are not gifts and, frankly, it's not about helping adoptive parents. I love my birth daughter's parents with all my heart, but I didn't get pregnant to give them a gift. I did what I felt was the right thing for my child.

The best part of my story is by far the relationship I have with my birth daughter. To illustrate this, let me tell you about our most recent visit.

I knocked on the door and three-year-old Rory was the first to greet me, jumping into my arms and squeezing me tight. She grabbed my hand and we ran up to her room where she showed me all her toys, books, and hair accessories. Then she decided that she needed to brush my hair and put every single bow she owned in it, because, "You can't have fancy hair unless there are ten bows." Then we played with toys and read stories and she talked about having a sleepover someday, how she wanted me to stay and play with her and read stories for a long, long, long, long time.

Then we went downstairs and I caught up with her adoptive mama while my husband played with her and her brothers. The kids put on a mini-talent show for us and we read even more stories. Then their daddy came home from work and it made my heart so happy to watch little Rory run up to him and throw her arms around him. She is a daddy's girl and he is one of the best dads I've ever met.

My heart was happy as I watched her interact with her family. I know she is safe and happy with them. When the time came to go, I picked her up and kissed her goodbye, telling her I'd come back and see her soon. Saying goodbye is always bittersweet, but I slept well that night knowing she was well-loved at home.

Adoptive parents reading this, I'm not here to steal your title of mother. We can both be very real moms in different ways, and that's okay. Please don't be threatened. Encourage a conversation about your child's birth parents with them - they deserve to know their story. They deserve to know their birth parents if that's what they need. Birth and adoptive parents should, whenever possible, work together to help the adoptee navigate their identity.

Adoptees: you don't *have* to be grateful. Some people will say, "Aren't you so grateful that you were adopted by such a good family?" Others will tell you that your birth parents placed you because they love you. That was true for me. I loved my child, so I did what I thought was best for her, and I think most adoptive families are great. But that doesn't mean you're not allowed to have hard feelings. Please don't be afraid to bring it up with your birth and adoptive families, or to seek professional help. No matter what anyone says, you can feel any way you want to about your adoption story; it's your experience and no one can tell you what your truth is.

APRIL

My name is April, and I am a thirty-eight-year-old homeschool teacher, worship leader and actor. I was the oldest child in my family, and my younger sister died in a car wreck when I was nine. My parents subsequently divorced, and my mom disappeared for a year and a half. I eventually went to live with my maternal grandparents, until we received notice that my mom was in jail in Missouri for drug smuggling, and we bailed her out and brought her home. She was raped within the next year by a boyfriend and became pregnant with another girl.

My grandparents kicked us out not long after my sister was born and we moved into some projects in Cedar Hill, Texas. My mother then married another man who had a closet meth addiction and he became physically abusive. We moved to Arlington, and he stalked us for a while. Then she met and married another man who was a Christian and a good man. Mom again got pregnant with my brother, but then her husband died in a car wreck on his way to work.

This caused me to spiral into drugs and depression and within months, I became pregnant with my son, who I placed for adoption at age fifteen. I found the Lord through this trial, and went on to graduate high school with honors, obtain my BA from UTA with a 3.97 GPA, and I have been working in education and the creative arts for the last fifteen years.

I chose to make an adoption plan because, at that time, I did not feel as if I had any means of support. My stepdad and provider had recently died, my mom was poor and uneducated, I was fifteen and in high school, and my extended family did not think I should keep the child. My maternal grandmother had previously forced my mom to have two abortions before she had me, and she and my other relatives thought my mom should have me sent away to a home for unwed pregnant teens. Thankfully, my mom chose to let me stay at home, but we never really discussed the possibility of me raising the baby. My mom was also pregnant with my little brother at the time, and we did not know how we were going to make it.

Everyone who knew about the adoption during and after was usually overwhelmingly positive, especially the adults and people at church. A few teen moms at the alternative school I was sent to made remarks to me about how they could never "give their babies away." At the time, I thought they were being selfish, but now I see it differently.

My sister had a son years later that my mom and new stepdad are currently raising, and in one time, in anger, she accused me of being jealous of her, and the fact that her son was still inside our family. I know she was mad and didn't mean it, but that is the most painful thing someone has ever said to me regarding the adoption.

Placing my child with others was by far the hardest thing I have ever gone through.

At its best, I tend to look at adoption through the biblical lens. Adoption is not even understood in many other cultures where children are left on the street to fend for themselves. I am thankful that we have a biblical basis in the West for understanding adoption, that it can be a good thing and that the rights of the adopted child are equal to those of the natural child, per Galatians 4:4-5 and Romans 8:15-16.

Still, the whole experience of placing my child with others was incredibly painful, and by far the hardest thing I have ever gone through. I can't really put it into words. I felt that it was my only option at the time, but I wish that I had had more support and encouragement to keep my baby. Everyone acted like the only loving thing to do was give him away, especially people in the church. As a new believer, I assumed

34

that they all knew better than me, because they were older and had known Jesus longer.

At fifteen, it was very difficult for me to think long-term, and to understand how things would change. I could only see my situation at the moment, which looked impossible. I wish I had lived in a country like Germany, which offers financial help, support, and job training to young moms to help them keep their babies. They don't even have an adoption process pre-birth in the UK; babies are only placed for adoption in cases of abandonment after birth. I would have never abandoned my baby; once I gave birth to him, letting him go to his new parents was the most excruciating moment of my life.

After the adoption, I began having panic attacks that were debilitating; I couldn't leave the house for over a month because every time I did, I would have a panic attack. It completely changed my ability to make friends - or to have healthy romantic relationships - for a very long time. The panic attacks subsided after about six or seven years, and marrying my husband also brought a lot of healing. Even though the adoption was open, I couldn't even see my son for two years because every time I did, it would launch me into a deep depression for at least a week afterwards.

However, when he was about three, I decided that the depression was worth it, I just wanted to see him, so I went through that for about ten years. He is twenty-two now and it is easier to see him and be with him, although it is still hard and emotionally difficult for my daughter as well. It has created a void in my family that we all have to deal with and struggle with in our own way. I can never replace the time I did not get to spend with him. He is my son, and I love him as much as I love my daughter. I would do anything for him, but he has other parents.

It is a huge misconception that birth parents don't care about the baby, that they are all irresponsible and selfish, that they shouldn't be encouraged to keep their baby and given support in order to help make that happen. The truth is, there is a tragic loss of identity that occurs through adoption. It should be the absolute last option. Women should be given every chance to keep their children, and if that is not possible, we should make every effort to keep children within the birth family so that this loss of identity does not occur.

The only way I survived the trauma of the adoption was through Jesus. He got me through it and has healed my heart in so many ways, but it was not easy. It still isn't easy.

I personally don't like the terms "bio-mom" or "bio-dad." They sound so technical. I actually prefer the phrase "first mom." It gives more honor to the fact that the child has a story and that the mom who carried them for nine months and gave birth to them was actually their mom, that that act of love and sacrifice is significant. I will always be my son's mom, even though a different mom raised him.

The best part of my adoption story is that I got to know Jesus through the pain and that my son is a beautiful, thriving, talented, incredible person. That I do get to have a relationship with him even though it is not what I wish it was. That God somehow works all things together for the good of those who love Him and are called according to His purpose.

To adoptees, I would say that your mom loves you so much more than you know. She may not be around or she may not know how to show it well, but she loves you more than life itself and did what she thought was best for you at the time, at great emotional cost to herself.

To adoptive parents, I would say that it is important to be aware that the best possible place for any child is with their natural family. There are many deep-seated psychological and spiritual reasons for this. Even if the birth family has issues, even if there are major problems that need to be worked through, adoption should only be considered in cases of abandonment, severe abuse, and neglect. This often does not occur until after birth, until kids are much older, which is why there is a push inside the church for young or unwed moms to "do the moral thing" and place their child with a "more suitable home," or to fill the demand for babies by families that cannot have them.

However, I would direct these families' attention to the story of Abraham and Sarah in Genesis 17. Although they were way past childbearing age, God promised them a son.

They became impatient with waiting, and tried to make the promise happen through other means, which led to pain and distress for their servant Hagar, as well as Abraham's first son, Ishmael. It is always better to wait for God's best, than to try to go outside of His perfect will and make things happen on our own. We will inevitably hurt people in the process.

AUBREY

Hi, my name is Aubrey. I'm twenty-six years old and work as a bridge designer for a civil engineering company in St. Louis, Missouri. I live with my boyfriend who does production for band tours and our two-year-old goldendoodle named Felix. I placed my daughter for adoption when I was nineteen years old, during my freshman year of college and have been on a journey to healing ever since. That has looked like a lot of things through the years, which is a much longer story, but has included struggling through college, then moving to Cincinnati, then Seattle, and finally back to my home state of Missouri. I am currently training to be a yoga teacher and spend most of my spare time reading books on chakras, cooking Mexican food, and finding a patio for drinks with my friends. My favorite color is yellow and my Myer's-Briggs personality is ENFP.

My adoption is open and always has been. "Open" can mean a lot of different things these days, and I think mine is on the more open side of the spectrum. My daughter lives in my hometown, as do my parents, so I spend quite a bit of time visiting home, and I get to visit my daughter nearly every time - and will be moving home here in a couple months which is extremely exciting! We go to the library, play at the park, go get frozen custard or Taco Tuesday or Italian - that girl *loves* her balsamic vinegar and bread! Or sometimes we just hang out around my parents' house picking up acorns or baking cookies. I have even had a few slumber parties with her!

She has always known I am her birth mom and speaks about it pretty freely and positively. She gets to play with my sibling's children, and has invited my parents to grand-parent's day events at her school. Her adoptive family's grandparents all died recently, so she was very happy to know Pat and Papa Joe were also her grandparents. The adoptive family has played a huge part in not just bringing my daughter into their family, but really creating an open sense of what family can mean and who all can be part of it. We all love and celebrate each other, which is better than any "open" adoption I could have dreamed of!

One little bit I love about our adoption story is that I was given the birth certificate in the hospital and was asked to fill it out. I was confused because I knew she was going to be named Brooklyn, but I wasn't sure if I should put her last name as mine (Price) or the adoptive family's, because she had been identified up to that point as "Baby Girl Price" on her hospital tags. The staff explained to me (not so well in detail) that it didn't matter, because she was going to get a new one when she was adopted anyway. Well, up until that point, we had been calling her Gator when I was pregnant (because she still had a little tail at the time, and I didn't like calling her "it"), and then "Ali-Gator" when we found out she was a girl.

So what did I put on the birth certificate that "didn't matter"? Well, "Ali Gator Price," of course! (Face palm.) As I mentioned, it took over a year for her adoption to be finalized, so all her insurance and legal paperwork had to refer to her as "Ali Gator Price." I was mortified! It has obviously been changed since, but I always wonder if she'll have to put that down on formal documentations that ask if you've ever gone by another name. Talk about embarrassing!

Adoption was the means to get my daughter out of a volatile situation and give her the best chance for a happy life. At nineteen, I did not have the education or experience to get a good job with stable hours and benefits like health insurance to provide for my child. Like every other birth-mother I have met, it started with a pregnancy in a less-than-ideal situation. I had just turned eighteen when I found out I was pregnant because of an unfortunate drunken mishap where no condom was involved and where I had taken Plan B the next morning. I knew the father was a guy I had been casually seeing. I was sad and confused, as I had dreams I was chasing of seeing the world and becoming an engineer, all of which seemed insurmountable with a child. To make matters worse, the father - who I first assumed was just an asshole (excuse the language) - was actually a deeply troubled, abusive partner. I wanted my daughter to have a loving mother and father and family like I had growing up, and I knew that her father and I would never be that family.

There have been plenty of positive comments from friends and family who love and support me and there have been the handful

Birthmothers put their child's best interests ahead of their own feelings and heartache.

of negative comments, mostly from people ignorant to the world of adoption. My one big thing is when people allude to the fact that I made the "right choice" by not getting an abortion - or even worse, use me as an example to push pro-life or religious ideals. Very few people know the despair of a young, unwed mother in an abusive relationship, and I can promise that I am forever thankful I had a choice. I *chose* adoption, but I almost didn't. Not because I didn't love my child, but because my abuser was holding the adoption

41

papers over my head as a means to force me to stay in a relationship.

When I tried to leave, he would threaten to take custody of our child because "his family had more money than mine and could afford a better lawyer." Our unborn child was a pawn in his manipulative arsenal. He broke me down, piece by piece, and what mother wants to bring their child into that kind of life? I did the very best I could to stay in a fake relationship with my abuser to convince him to sign the papers, and thankfully for all of us, he did. But it took over a year for the adoption to be finalized (thank you, state of Missouri). All the while, he could have taken custody of our daughter at any point if I had made him mad enough. So I walked on eggshells and lost my very sense of self to an abusive relationship until it was finally safe for our daughter and for me to leave.

The thing about adoption is no woman is a birthmother because everything is sunshine and roses - instead, there is ALWAYS heartache, trauma, abuse, and neglect right on the other side of the door. But the largest misconception I see portrayed is that birth parents "gave up" their children. You've gotta love Hollywood for all the literal dumping of babies in boxes or baskets outside of fire stations. Every birthmother I have met chose adoption for their child be-cause they loved them more than anything. Every. Single.

One. Birthmothers put their child's best interests ahead of their own feelings and heartache.

I wish that people understood there is a very dark side to adoption. Statistics show over eighty percent of women who place their children for adoption develop depression. Many suffer from secondary infertility and birthmothers are more likely to commit suicide. On social media, and in stories, I mostly speak to the positives of how much I love my daughter, how much I love her family and how our relationship has morphed into something amazing over time. And I truly feel all these things!

But the other side are deep wounds from abuse, the loss of my child, years of depression and self-medicating and then prescribed medication, loneliness and not feeling accepted or understood. It is *so* hard, and there are very few resources out there or people who advocate for birthmothers. It's a hard topic to ford, because while I want to share some of these nitty-gritty details to maybe help others understand situations surrounding birthmothers, I am hesitant to share because I know one day my daughter will have access to all these things I am saying. How will she feel to hear these stories of her birth father being a monster? Do I want her to have to face those publicly, or in privacy when she is old enough to understand?

I will never not be looking out for her best interests, and that sometimes means sharing less so her story is hers alone, and not public knowledge. But, for the general public, I want them to understand that there are a lot of complex emotions involved with being a birthmother, so please don't push the line "to think on the bright side because you gave your child a better life." Yes, we know - that is why we did it, but we still need to be allowed to feel the sorrow and loss that go right along with it. If you're an adoptee, I would just say that whatever your story may be, I can bet you that your birthmother loves you more than anything and has always wanted - and will always want - what is best for you.

BROOKLYN

In my case, age didn't really play a large part in choosing to make an adoption plan. I was induced on my thirty-second birthday, so age wasn't a large factor in the decision-making process. Also, there's this misconception about birth parents that we didn't love our children. But while it was never my intention to have children, I'm so glad that I did! I know adoption isn't always sunshine and rainbows all the time, but my heart has grown and been so full since my daughter and her adoptive parents came into my life.

I felt it was in my baby's best interest to be raised by two Christian parents in a loving relationship that could provide for her needs better than I could. But I would say that my adoption is very open. My daughter's adoptive parents have become part of my family, and we go to church together every week, so I don't think it gets much more open!

I want others to know how amazing my experience has been! I want other women who are considering placing their babies for adoption to understand that adoption doesn't have to be as scary as it was in days of old. These days, you can still place your child for adoption and still have a relationship with them.

Experts and agencies are advocating for open adop-tions, and I think that takes away a lot of the sting that is

The more people to love on a child, the better.

typically associated with placing a child. I was able to give an amazing couple the opportunity to be parents, which is what they wanted more than anything else in the world. That feeling alone has been wonderful! I've been able to be an active part of my daughter's life, and the whole thing has truly been a blessing in my life!

I'm not sure what the best thing someone has said to me about adoption is, but I know what the worst thing is. My best friend told me after my daughter was legally adopted that he wished I had put more thought into raising the baby myself. It really rained on my parade that he said that as I was so happy with how everything had turned out. Also, I'm not a big fan of the term "put(ting) up for adoption." I prefer "placed for adoption." Not everyone is meant to be a parent, so I'm thankful for the people out there who are willing to raise and love children as their own, even if they don't share the same genes.

I would tell adoptees to rest assured that it wasn't that they were placed for adoption because their parents didn't love them - it was because they loved them so much and wanted them to have everything they deserved. To adoptive parents, I would say, "Thank you for loving our biological children the same way we as biological parents do!"

The best part of my adoption story is the way everything has turned out. My family has grown exponentially, and it was like a match made in Heaven. I have a beautiful little girl in my life who is being raised by two amazing adoptive parents who also love her to the moon and back. The more people to love on a child, the better, and that is absolutely the case with our very modern family!

CAMILA

I have been called many things throughout my life. Some true, some untrue. But among all the words, I am a birth mother. I have navigated this often taboo title for sixteen years now. I was only fourteen when I became pregnant and fifteen years old at delivery and my options were few. I was told that if I chose to parent, I didn't have a home to stay in. I was promiscuous because I lived a life not everyone could fathom. I numbed my pain with drugs and alcohol and boys and, in the end, was taken advantage of by a grown man.

But I overcame. I am not the person I was when I became pregnant. I have grown and healed. My daughter quite literally saved my life...perhaps it wasn't the way anyone would plan redemption, but God authored it into my story and gave me a voice loud enough to help others who may need to hear what all I was able to overcome. Only fourteen and a product of statutory rape, I made the hardest decision of my life, mostly alone. What parental involvement I had was hardly supportive, paired with an abusive home life, and I knew the only option that would benefit this innocent life was one that would break my own heart.

Our adoption was open but I wasn't sure to what degree until my birth daughter's parents reached out to me. We visited when she turned one and after that I received pictures every year around her birthday. I physically ached for the loss I felt but didn't realize we had any other options.

Adoption meant a better opportunity at life for my daughter. She didn't ask to be conceived and born into such a toxic situation. I was young and naive, grossly manipulated and used, and she was perfect, undeserving of any of that.

When adoption was presented to me, it broke my heart to admit that I wasn't what was best for her because she was the best thing that had ever happened to me.

I fought through a living hell to place her in the arms of a family I chose.

Kids can be cruel. I went to a very large high school, but because there was a school in the area only for pregnant teens, I was not only the *only* pregnant student that year but I was also the new girl and a freshman. None of these people knew me but many were quick to make assumptions. I was called a ho, a slut, and once I returned to school and had to answer questions about my baby, some peers told me how cruel it was to "just give your baby away." It was a lonely place to be surrounded by so many people.

As an adult, I've spoken to crowds, shared my story, and I write from my social media outlets and blog. I have been told time and time again how brave I was, how selfless I was, but I still remember the sting of every hurtful comment spat out by people who didn't know my situation or my heart.

I hate the phrase "given up." I don't give anything up and especially not my child. I fought through a living hell to place her in the arms of a family I chose...a family to love her in ways that I couldn't.

I want people to know that most of us aren't as scary as we've been portrayed. We won't try to take our child back if you invite us into their life. We often hurt from the loss of parenthood but are so grateful for every moment we get invited into. I know I'm not "mom," but I'm just thankful to be around.

My story is one of redemption. I was given a second chance, and in the hopes of having a relationship with her one day, I wanted to be a person she would want to know.

To adoptees and adoptive parents, I'd say that communication is key. Be honest, upfront and painfully truthful. Walk this road together to keep all hearts whole. When space is needed from any side, vocalize that too. Relationships are not always easy and an open adoption is no exception. Walk into it with unconditional love and a willingness to communicate.

DESIRAE

I was born and raised in Montana, I have had a lot of struggles in my life, and I have been my own worst enemy. When I get down on myself, I try my hardest to remind myself how far I have come and how hard I have had to fight to get there. I wanted my kids to have the opportunity to know me, my family and their siblings…on their time.

My first child was born when I was sixteen, and I don't know if I would say he was the hardest decision to make. But I had him in my room for three days and I wanted to keep him so bad. I was told how hard it would be to parent at sixteen, and it seemed impossible. The family I had chosen was amazing, and I didn't doubt for a second that he would be loved and have an amazing life. It still broke my heart, but I knew that they would always be there for me.

I have five kids, four of whom I placed for adoption by families. Each adoption has gone differently. And regardless of the outcome, I am blessed to know that my children were all given amazing lives and have families that love them. My wish is to have all the kids and all the parents together one day in a reunion of sorts. We were almost there recently - we got to see everyone all together for a family wedding. The love, joy, and laughter that was shared and the respect given was amazing. We were just short one middle son and his family from this reunion. So here is to us all watching him play baseball someday. With his family included.

The best thing I've been told about placing my children was that it was a selfless act of love and that I had a hand in creating not one but *five* amazing families. The worst thing I've been told is that I am heartless and I must have never loved my kids, that I should have aborted.

I think expectant moms are afraid that they will never see their child again. It is really hard to hold your child in your arms and hand them over to people you don't know very well. But, as a parent, you can choose the adoption plan you want. You can choose the type of family you want raising your child, helping create a family. One that is different and unique in its own beautiful way.

The biggest misconception about being a birth parent is that the adoptive family will never let you have contact with your child and that they don't want a relationship between mother and child. I have found mostly the opposite. My middle son, his mom has been the most difficult. She has told him none of us wanted anything to do with him, which is so far from the truth. I don't know exactly what story he has ben told about his adoption, but I am guessing he doesn't know the truth.

I wish people could know that my life was a mess a lot of the time, and I knew that I couldn't drag my children through it. My youngest daughter has been through enough because of me. I want people to understand that I love my kids with my whole heart and that I only wanted the best life for them.

My mom was adopted, and this poem was given to her by her adopted mom. It has had such an incredible impact on my life:

> "Once there were two women
> Who never knew each other.
> One you do not remember,

The other you call mother.
Two different lives
Shaped to make yours one.
One became your guiding star,
The other became your sun.

The first gave you life
And the second taught you to live it.
The first gave you a need for love
And the second was there to give it.
One gave you a nationality,
The other gave you a name.
One gave you a seed of talent,
The other gave you an aim.

One gave you emotions,
The other calmed your fears.
One saw your first sweet smile,
The other dried your tears.
One gave you [life] -
It was all that she could do.
The other prayed for a child
And God led her straight to you.

And now you ask me
Through your tears,

The age-old question
Through the years:
Heredity or environment
Which are you the product of?
Neither, my darling - neither,
Just two different kinds of love."

- Author Unknown

I love my kids with my whole heart...
I only wanted the best life for them.

To adoptees, I would say to please try to remember that the mom who [placed you], it was the hardest decision of her life. Don't feel she didn't love you, she did it out of love. Her heart broke making the decision. Take that into consideration and give her a chance to tell you why. Remember, she handpicked your parents, they were chosen just for you.

To adoptive parents...please don't feel that, if your child asks about their birth parents, don't feel it as a knock toward you. They love you and that will never change. Open your heart to an expanded family that will just show your child more love. It takes a village...or just one large, united family.

I think adoption has become very clear to me lately. As I was able to watch my now-grown kids with their beautiful families and seeing the joy on their faces...that completes it all for me. Watching my daughter have her father/daughter dance at her wedding. Seeing my oldest son with a huge smile with his new fiancée as his parents looked on with joy. Watching my daughter I raised with a smile on her face to be around family. Watching my youngest son and his parents become a closer part of my family. These things are what adoption is about. Giving life and love to a child and watching it grow into this huge family...when they are ready.

ERICA

Author's Note: Erica Shaw specifically requested to use her real name. Instagram: @eriquita

My name is Erica and I've been a birth mom for over eleven years now. My pregnancy was something I kept pretty private for many years before I started having a deep desire to share about it. I started going to therapy a few years after I had my daughter and that truly changed my life and positively affected the entire adoption experience.

I don't know what my relationship would be with all the people involved in this adoption without having gone to therapy. It helped me gain clarity and my desire to share about my experience really came from that. Now I write about it on social media and I've done things like podcast interviews and some public speaking.

I had just turned twenty, so my age DEFINITELY affected my decisions, or lack thereof. I was just a baby back then. Because I lacked life experience, I couldn't foresee what was to come and what I might want to plan for. It also was just so traumatic that I couldn't see past the moment I was in. I couldn't see past the hospital. And I also lacked the self-confidence to trust my instincts and to speak up. It would be very different if it happened to me now as a thirty-one-year-old.

I knew I wanted an open adoption but that was all I really laid out. I knew I wanted to be involved in her life, so that was part of the conversation from the beginning. But it was really hard for me to look down the road and try to anticipate what I would want later on and very hard to take myself out of my present circumstance.

The best thing someone said to me is something my therapist taught me: "Adoption is about the *and*." It is both hard *and* a gift. It is selfless *and* selfish. It is light *and* dark. It is life *and* loss. I hold on to that and it has given

Adoption does not end at the hospital, even though that's how movies show it.

me so much peace. The worst thing I've heard was someone equating it to an abortion. Adoption is multifaceted to me, a never-ending cycle. I say it can feel almost unbearably painful, but also a breathtaking gift that keeps on giving.

I want people to understand that being a birth parent is a journey of ups and downs that never end. There's so much to learn and navigate. It's also very individual, and everyone experiences it differently, so it can feel very isolating because it feels like no one can understand what you're going through. I also want people to know that they can ask me as many questions as they want; I love to talk about it (even if I cry). It's healing for me but I also really want to spread awareness of what it's like to be a birth parent.

One of the biggest misconceptions is that this decision leaves you with no regrets. I don't ever regret choosing life, but sometimes I regret choosing adoption. And that's just a part of my journey that I have to navigate. It's a part of my "and." I want to note that the regret I feel has NOTHING to do with my daughter's adopted family. They are wonderful and she has a great life with them. It has everything to do with *my own* desire to parent and be with my baby at all times.

Again, I wish people could understand that there are contradictions in adoption - the "and." That I can feel *two* things at once about it. And that adoption is not something neat and tidy that's wrapped in a bow. It's not a complete answer or solution. It's all the things I said above: it's painful and it's beautiful. Along with that, adoption does not end at the hospital, even though that's how movies show it. That is only the beginning - the rest of life has yet to be lived after that.

I honestly hate any of the birth parent phrases I hear. They make me cringe. I don't like the term "birth mom" because I *am* a mom! A *different* kind of mom. I get the need for it, it's a descriptor for clarity, but it just doesn't sit well with me. I don't like "Birthmother's Day" being the day before Mother's Day either. It doesn't feel special to me...it feels heartbreaking. The only thing coming to mind as far as phrases I love is the sound of my daughter saying my name.

My daughter is the best part of my story. Hands down. She is light and love and sass but also sweetness. I love her more than anything and it is such a profound blessing to know her. I don't know if I could handle adoption without knowing her.

At the end of the day, I would tell adoptees and adoptive parents to go to therapy. Preferably to a therapist with experience surrounding adoption, or at least loss.

Work through your stuff, have a safe space to say the deep dark things that creep in. A place where you can cultivate resilience and light. Work on vulnerability. Communicate with the birth parents. Speak your fears and insecurities and hopes and desires and questions to each other.

Lastly, it's okay to feel two (of what should be opposite) things at once. You can be happy *and* sad. I am! I am happy and sad. I feel love *and* I feel loss. And it's okay.

KELSEY

My name's Kelsey and I'm thirty-one years old. I have been married for almost four years and have a three-year-old daughter. I come from a wonderful, caring family in central Texas. After high school, I went on to college and obtained my Undergraduate and Master's in Social Work. It was always my goal to work in the adoption field, specifically with birth mothers, which I have now been doing for six years. I worked with birth mothers for four years and have worked with adoptive parents now for almost two years. I was inspired to work in adoption after I experienced an unplanned pregnancy and placed my daughter for adoption when I was eighteen years old.

Due to my age, I was not financially independent - or independent at all for that manner. Being seventeen when I got pregnant and eighteen when I had her, I did not have any resources to fall back on, only my parents. This played a significant role in my decision to make an adoption plan since I did not have the personal means to parent a child, nor the maturity.

I remember when I was pregnant, I had some people who told me the child would always hate me for placing her for adoption. To be honest though, I haven't gotten many bad reactions when I have shared my story. It has been many years since anyone has said anything bad to me about my adoption plan. I would imagine people have thought things but they have not said them to me.

Adoption is something that I have always been familiar with. My mother was adopted along with her brother and we always knew about adoption. In fact, the agency I work for is where they were adopted from. I was seventeen and a senior in high school when I found out I was pregnant. I was not in a firm relationship with the father of the child, nor was I mature enough to raise a child on my own or a child at all at that time. Before I had confirmed I was pregnant, I knew if I was, I would be making an adoption plan.

I also recognized that if I were to try to parent, it would not be me parenting this child but my parents. This is not something they wanted, nor did I want that for them or my child.

I also wanted more for my child. I wanted them to have a two-parent household, parents who could provide the life for her that I had growing up and not the struggles she would have with a teenage parent who had no idea how to take care of herself, let alone a child. I also had goals for myself that would not be reachable were I to have parented her, such as college.

The biggest misconception about birth parents is that we are scary, want our children back, or that we would attempt to regain the role of mother.

I think to me, adoption means opportunity. And that is opportunity for the whole adoption triad, but I think it also extends beyond the triad into family members and their own communities. It is opportunity for birth parents to fulfill their hopes and dreams while also allowing better opportunities for their child. It is opportunity for the adoptee to have what the birth mother could not provide, like a two-parent household, stable home life, and better financial upbringing. It is opportunity for the adoptive parents to be parents to a child and continue that cycle of opportunity for someone.

In thinking about how it is opportunity for others, it's opportunity to be a sister, uncle, grandparent, and friend to someone who is adopted and honoring their unique story. It's also opportunity to console your grieving friend who just placed her child for adoption and to sit with her in her grief that is so unknown to you. It's an opportunity to grow as a friend to someone going through the adoption process and sitting with them in their fears that they will never become parents.

My adoption is semi-open, meaning I have received picture and letter updates on my daughter through the agency. This is something that has worked great for me, and I would have never known any different until working in the adoption field and learning there are different options for people.

I can think of two things that people have said that really meant a lot to me. I was attending a birth mother's support group at the agency. During our group, two girls shared that my testimonial in one of the agency brochures they received had changed their adoption experience and been a sense of comfort and motivation for them. They also shared that when they had seen me walk in the room, they thought, "Oh my gosh, she is a real person. Her story is real."

There was also another time recently at a family's adoption finalization that an adoptive family shared with me that I had impacted their experience as well. Years ago, when they were at our new family orientation, I had spoken on the birth mother panel. They explained that my story really impacted them and made a difference in how they feel about birth mothers and the adoption process. They thanked me for having the bravery to share my story.

That does not mean my experience was easy by any means, and I truly hope that the stigma of it being "an easy way out" will end. I may be in a great place now but in the beginning, it was so hard. I had my daughter in July and the next month, I left for college. The first few years, I was really stuck in my grief and almost quit college my first year so I could go back to the comfort of my home.

When I think back on it now, I can't imagine what this time was also like for my own parents, watching their daughter go through something so hard and unique and not know how to comfort her. Being a birth mother can feel pretty isolating since it's a grief that is so different from others. I can liken it to a death but it's different because it's not final; it's very unknown and questioning as well.

I also want others to know that it's okay to ask about a birth mother's experience or the child she placed. Ignoring it gives the impression that it never happened, which is not the case. The birth mother will always remember this child and is happy to know that others also remember and are curious about how they are doing.

The biggest misconception about birth parents is that we are scary, want our children back, or that we would attempt to regain the role of mother. There is still a lack of education out there regarding adoption and these are also fears I hear even in the professional world of adoption. If anything, most birth parents want to maintain boundaries and a level of respect to the adoptive parents. They do not want to ruin the relationship that they have and they want it to be successful long-term.

Birth parents understand they are not the parents and they are not trying to be parents. They just want to know that the adoptive parents love their child, that they are happy, and that their child is happy. They also want the adoptive parents they chose and their child to be proud of the person they became. For them all to know that they did not place for nothing, that they (the birth parents) made something of themselves afterwards.

I wish people could understand that even though I come from a well-to-do and supportive family who could have made a parenting plan work, I chose adoption for good reasons. I sometimes fear that people may question why I made my plan, or they won't understand why - but it makes so much sense to me. Sure, my family could have made it work, but that's not the life I wanted for my child, for me, or my parents. That decision would have affected everyone in my family, not just me or my daughter.

I feel peace knowing that my daughter is where she was meant to be and she is happy, and that her family is happy she is a part of their lives.

LINDIE

I am a twenty-five-year-old birthmother, a senior majoring in child development, and I have an eight-month-old daughter I placed for adoption at birth. I love the beach, hiking, and blogging.

I didn't find out I was pregnant until I was five months along. The birthfather was someone who I had only briefly dated. I had just started dating another man who I knew I wanted to marry. I wasn't ready to be a mother to a stranger's child.

I was twenty-four when I placed my daughter for adoption. I relinquished my rights at the hospital to her adoptive parents who I had matched with several months before. I knew I didn't want to be a single mother who couldn't provide for her child. I hadn't even finished college yet. I wanted to be selfish and keep her because I had always wanted to be a mother, but I knew that wasn't what was best for my daughter. I love children. I put aside my own wants and feelings so my child could have a better life.

Many people have reached out and been extremely supportive about my adoption plan. They express gratitude and say I changed the adoptive parents' lives for the better. Others have been extremely judging; they looked at me like there was something wrong with me. They acted like I was a horrible person.

It's hard. It's difficult, carrying this baby inside of you and then handing it over to someone else. At no point did I *not* want my daughter. I loved and wanted her so badly that I knew I had to make a decision for her to have the best life possible, which - devastatingly - was placing her for adoption.

There is also the misconception that our children were taken by social services because we put them in danger.

Some people think that we birth parents hate our babies. Or that we don't want our children. Though there is also the misconception that our children were taken by social services because we put them in danger.

I hate it when people say, "You're such a good person because you chose life, everyone should choose life." I made a decision that worked for me and one I knew I could handle. Others should be able to choose whatever they need, too. It makes me happy that adoption and birthmothers are being talked about more, in general.

I am so proud of both adoptees and adoptive parents. Adoption causes so many emotions and they deal with that their whole lives. As a birthmother, I carry different emotions towards adoption than adoptees or adoptive parents.

My daughter has so many people who love her. Her adoptive parents love her, and I love her. We are a big family who all want what's best for her. They've also accepted me as family and are constantly showing me their love and support.

It's hard to find words to explain exactly what adoption means to me. Adoption is so important and intricate. Because of adoption, I know my daughter has loving, stable parents who can provide her with everything she needs. I love her more than anything else in the world.

MONIQUA

I'm a twenty-nine-year-old massage therapist living in the beautiful state of Michigan. I love kayaking, tacos, hiking, my two kitties, and anything purple. I just recently bought my first home and fulfilled my lifelong dream of having a beautiful, purple front door! My beautiful baby boy turned six in May, and he is the most precious thing I hold inside of my heart.

I was twenty-two, turned twenty-three while pregnant, and the father wanted nothing to do with the situation. Living in a studio apartment, working two jobs... I was barely making ends meet for myself despite all my efforts to get ahead. It wasn't really my age that affected my decision, but more so where I was at in life. Trying to become this adult and the fact that I wanted my baby to have two loving parents.

My son deserved two parents to love and support him. He deserved to have parents that could be present, not configuring daycares or babysitters while watching his mom struggle just to afford the necessities. He deserved life experiences and fun adventures and financial stability. He deserved the home I wanted more than anything to give to him but wasn't able to give despite all my efforts.

The adoption is very open. He has known exactly who I am since day one. He knows my family, I can visit whenever time allows, and he proudly talks about me. When he was barely four years old, he even told a random lady at Panera he came from my tummy. The couple I placed my son with have been my extremely close friends for almost eight years, a couple years prior to when I became pregnant.

To me, adoption means having a chance - a real chance at a full and happy life. It means more opportunities for my baby, *quadruple* the love for my baby. And hopefully less of a struggle to achieve *his* goals and dreams.

I've heard the typical remarks about placing my child for adoption: "How selfish of you..." etcetera. But in all honesty, I have had SUCH an incredible support system from so many different avenues. I've received a lot of love and respect and have people by my side.

My birth parent experience has been a lot of things. It's beautiful. It's messy. It's painful. It's joyful. The grief comes in waves. It will hit you out of nowhere. There is not a day that goes by that my beautiful baby isn't on my mind. The first year is the absolute hardest, and you will forever walk around with this hole in your heart, this hole in your soul. It never goes away, except when your baby is in your arms, even if for a moment.

The grief comes in waves. It will hit you out of nowhere.

The biggest misconception about birth parents is that we don't care. That we are promiscuous, that we are uneducated deadbeats, that we are taking "the easy way out." That's *far* from the truth. I cared so much, I made the hardest decision of my life. I was twenty-two, in a relationship with his birth father, graduated from massage school and had been working as a nanny to three beautiful babies from the time the oldest was a newborn, while getting my feet planted in a massage career. Paying all my own bills, paying off my student loans, working hard to create a life for myself. I can assure you, placing my baby into the arms of another just a few days after I brought him into this world was THE hardest thing I have done in my life. In no way was that the easy way out. But everything has been decided out of complete and total love for our babies.

I want people to understand that you would do anything and everything to give your child the best life possible, even if that means having to shatter your own heart and place them into the loving arms of another family to do so.

I absolutely hate the term "giving up" or "gave away." I didn't give my baby away like an old pair of jeans. I placed my child into a loving home after much thought, many tears, and so many sleepless nights. I gave love. I gave life. But I never gave away - I placed.

The best part of my adoption story is how open it is. I don't have to hide it or feel ashamed. My baby boy knows he came from my tummy, and it's never been something that was hidden or that he has made to feel ashamed of. He didn't lose a family with this adoption. He knows my family; he has visits at my grandparent's house with my parents, he's met my cousins and aunts and uncles. I got to throw him a first birthday party at my parents' house with all of my family. I love that he didn't lose a family rather than gained an incredibly huge circle of love and support.

To adoptees: I can't speak for everyone, but I can almost certainly guarantee that you have not left the minds and hearts of your birth parents. Your wellbeing and happiness was at the root of our decision and we wanted to give everything in this world that, for some reason, we didn't feel like we could provide. There is nothing but love and respect for you at the root of our choice; we broke our own hearts to fill yours with all the love and opportunity in the world.

NORA

I'm a twenty-eight–year-old birth mom of eight years to a beautiful little girl. I'm a wife and mother who rarely misses an opportunity to cut a rug. I'm a graduate of the University of Florida with a degree in Public Relations. If I'm not spending my free time with family, you can typically find me exploring town or enjoying time with my close friends.

I was nineteen when I became pregnant and the birth father and I were not in a position to parent. My age was a big factor as I felt I was still a child myself. I had just finished my freshman year of college and knew I would not be able take care of her in the ways she deserved. I knew I wanted my daughter to grow up in a home with two parents who love each other, because without love, there is no compromise. She deserved the life I knew I could not give her.

It's been a long journey to say the least. There have been highs and lows, but one thing's for sure: I do not regret my decision. It hasn't always been easy, and at times it can be difficult to not get caught up in the "what ifs," but overall my experience has been positive. My birth daughter's family is wonderful and it's such a joy getting to watch her grow up, even if it's from a distance since the adoption is semi-open.

The best thing that has been said to me about adoption is in regards to how much of a sacrifice it is. It's not an easy decision to make, and I think that accurately describes the emotion and heaviness that comes with adoption. It is a sacrifice for everyone involved, and as difficult as adoption can be sometimes, the beauty of it is not lost on me. To me, adoption means redemption. The worst thing that has been said to me is that making that decision was "lazy and selfish."

That's the biggest misconception I hear about birth parents: that we are selfish, lazy, addicts, unloving, mentally unstable, volatile, just overall bad moms. As an advocate for birth moms, it can be very upsetting to see people paint birth

Without love, there is no compromise.

parents out as these monsters. Yes, some birth parents might struggle more than others, but what's important is that they recognized their shortcomings and knew they couldn't allow their child to grow up in that environment for whatever reason.

I didn't place my birth daughter because I didn't love her. I placed her because I did. It broke my heart to think that she would grow up without two parents in a committed relationship who wouldn't be able to provide for her in every

71

way. It was my hope that she wouldn't want for anything and be able to grow up watching two parents love her and each other. I think about her every day. I feel a huge responsibility to her to make sure I am the best person I can be. My story is ever-changing but I will never stop loving her or missing her.

I think the best part of my story is that I get to educate others and be an advocate for all sides of the triad. Although my story is certainly far from over, I look forward to what's in store.

To other members of the triad: We must advocate for one another. We cannot do this life without community and it is imperative we actively pursue education and support. Adoptive parents need to be on time with the updates. Those updates can mean the difference between sanity and insanity for a birth parent like me.

Also, ask questions, don't assume things. That applies to both adoptive parents and adoptees. If we do not ask those hard questions, we will get nowhere. Don't let fear dictate how you handle certain situations. Love adoptees well. Support them, encourage them. Adoptees need to not be scared to reach out for support and that starts at home with the parents. They are our children, our future.

REAGAN

I am a freelance photographer and part of a pet therapy team. I grew up in a small town and am still a tomboy at heart. I have had an open adoption for over twenty-one years now.

I chose adoption for selfish *and* selfless reasons. I knew I couldn't provide him with a stable home. I wanted to join the military and being a single mom would have ended that dream. I also wanted my unborn child to have the best chance at life possible.

I wish people could understand that I wasn't *coerced* into placing. That's why I don't like terms like "real parents" or "gave up my child." I prefer "placed for adoption." In fact, I made the decision on my son with my parents supporting me.

The best thing about it all was having my birth son tell me how thankful he was for me giving him his life.

Placing my child for adoption was the hardest decision of my life. It was a hard decision because I wanted a son and I was old enough that I should have been able to parent. But I

73

also know it was the best decision for both of us. Adoption is hard. But adoption also means love.

The best thing about it all was having my birth son tell me how thankful he was for me giving him his life. The relationship that I have with my birth son has been the best thing to come out of all this. He is one of my best friends.

The worst thing was having another birthmother tear me apart for sharing my story and not hating adoption like she did. Also, other people assume that we are all young, drug addicts, or dangerous to our children. We are not perfect. We are just people.

SAMANTHA

Today, I am a PTO president, member of our church leadership, former beauty queen, wife, full-time mother to two, and a regular volunteer in the community. I am also a birth mom to a fifteen-year-old.

I wasn't a teenager and I didn't come from a troubled home. I had lots of experience with children and was not without resources. I wasn't suffering from any type of addiction and had never even used alcohol or drugs, so to lots of people, I think they couldn't understand why I wouldn't choose to parent myself. While I knew I could raise my birth daughter, I also knew that I could not raise her the way she deserved. I wanted more for her. I wanted better.

When I looked at the big picture of parenting, I saw a life that would put her in a situation with a birth father that was abusive, had trouble with the law, and was controlled by his substance addiction twenty-four/seven. Taking away all his rights would be an uphill battle, and even if that did happen by a very slim margin, as a single mom, I knew that would leave me putting her in a daycare barely getting by and never seeing her. She deserved so much better than that life.

I loved this child so much for her not to have two parents that would always be there, keep her safe, show her respect, make sure her needs were taken care of, provide a shoulder to cry on and arms to hold her. The only path that gave her what she deserved was adoption, so there was always a sense of peace with this plan.

From the very first visit with the adoptive parents when I was pregnant, we talked about communication and having an open adoption. The first few years after placement seemed to be open with frequent letters, emails, gifts and the occasional phone call and visits.

At about five years in, there was a sudden change. This was the year that I got married, so I often wonder if that played a role in the change to communication, but letters became a bi-yearly thing and gifts and phone calls stopped altogether. Visits also became sporadic and took place randomly every couple years, which wouldn't have bothered me as much if the other forms of communications had stayed open. Now at fifteen years in, I long for those bi-yearly letters from ten years back.

I think it's assumed that we don't want to talk about our birth children.

Today, there is still some communication, so I consider my adoption semi-open but the one thing I wish I had done differently was at that very first meeting put a firm communication plan in place.

I really hope that in a few years, once she turns eighteen, things will change with the lack of communication, but realistically, I also know that this is the way it been for so long that it may never change.

What does adoption mean to me? This should be such a simple answer but nothing about adoption is simple. The short answer is adoption means love. Love beyond measure, beyond time, and beyond all else. The love for my daughter gave me the ability to forgo my own wants, needs, and desires to ensure hers were met. This love also caused a lot of hurt to so many. Adoption is a bittersweet journey with the highest highs and the lowest lows. It is not a journey that has a deadline but instead encompasses a lifetime.

Bottom line: words hurt. It doesn't matter if it's a stranger, a casual acquaintance, or even friends and family. I have had some of the harshest comments said to me by all of these:

- "You don't love your kid because you gave up on them."
- "I am glad you can teach others the worst thing in your life can just be a mistake and you can move on."
- "So when can we sign these adoption papers and get this over with already?"

It blows me away that people think they can say these types of things, but they do. They blurt them out as if they are obvious statements about all of us birth moms and like I should be okay with it because aren't we birth moms just "looking for an easy way out?"

I really believe that it is a lack of knowledge about adoption that causes a lot of this. I also believe that a lot of it is people just need to think before they speak, but wouldn't it be great if people knew that birth moms are usually older, sometimes have higher education, that they want to give their child a better future than they can provide, and they are so in love with this child.

On the other side of the coin, the kindest thing said to me was just a simple statement: "Tell me about your birth daughter."

I think it's assumed that we don't want to talk about our birth children but, in fact, it is just the opposite. We are *bursting* to share about what amazing people our birth children are and to have someone acknowledge their presence in our lives.

Adoption is a LIFETIME of emotions. I can still feel guilt, sadness, anger, hurt, and have bad days. After fifteen years, it may sound silly that I still have these, but I do. These emotions are not always there, but they still show up and it is like a gut punch that knocks the wind out of me when they do. It takes every ounce of me not to throw in the towel and say, "Enough! I change my mind!" I have to remind myself that the reason I have these days is because of how much I love her. It's how I cope. It doesn't change life and create a different outcome, but it is the one thing that I can hold on to that I have full control of: my love for her.

That love is what let me make hard decision after hard decision after hard decision. Not just to place, but to continue this path even if it means having my heartbreak over and over again. Bad days will always have a way of rearing up, but the love will always stay the same.

I got pregnant at twenty, so I was at an age where I was on my own and had just begun to start experiencing the world and the consequences of the world. I absolutely think that led to me having a better understanding and being able to see a fuller picture when making a choice. Knowing women of all ages, socioeconomic backgrounds, and circumstances have chosen adoption, it's still no surprise to me that the average birth mom age is twenty-two. Until the frontal lobe is fully developed, a person won't have a very clear sense of the reality of tomorrow or the needs of another person, so your choices are made mainly on instinct, which, of course, dictates *not* to

When we placed our child, we placed a piece of our hearts.

separate from your offspring. It makes it that much more amazing when you think of some of the young girls that have this foresight already.

What do I think are the biggest misconceptions about birth parents?

- That we will try to take our children back
- That our birth children were unwanted/unloved
- That we are very young
- That we are drug addicts
- That we are all poor
- That we are uneducated
- That we are unstable
- That we all have mental illness
- No support from the birth father
- That we are all belong in a *Lifetime*-type movie

I loathe the term "give up" and "gave away." Other phrases that make my blood boil:

- "What a great *present/gift* you gave that family."
- "Real family"
- "Gotcha day"
- "Adopting is so easy/you can always just adopt."
- "You have/will have other kids."
- "You aren't a mom."

The thing that I want to scream from the mountaintops is always just that I LOVED her when I was pregnant, I LOVED her when I placed, I LOVE her now, and I will LOVE her always.

The best part of my adoption story is seeing all the people that love my birth daughter. She is loved by her parents, her birth parents, her siblings, birth siblings, grandparents/aunts/uncles/etcetera, on all sides of the adoption triad. It is so amazing to see so much unconditional love just pour out for your birth child. Nothing will ever erase that love.

To adoptees, please PLEASE know that you were always wanted, always loved, always given everything we could, but you were never "given up."

To adoptive parents, I would say we are afraid of how powerless we are in this relationship. Every action we make around you is played out multiple times in our heads before acting on them for fear that we will do something that will make you take away the contact we do get. We will always grieve. We are at peace with our decisions but when we placed our child, we placed a piece of our hearts.

We aren't asking for sympathy but understanding that this is always with us. Please respect us. We get that this is a tricky relationship that doesn't come with an instruction manual, but please remember the trust we had to have in you when we placed our baby in your arms and said goodbye, and in return, give us that same trust back. Lastly, we are people, just like you.

SARAH

Author's Note: Sarah Noelle Schmidth did not wish to remain anonymous. She is the founder of Adoption Education Keys and you can find out more of her work at sunshine-in-a-bottle.com.

I am thirty-seven years old, married to the love of my life, and we parent our two-year-old son. I am also a birth mother to two amazing teenagers I placed with the same couple in 2001 and 2003.

All I ever wanted growing up was to be a wife and a mother. But I knew in the space of my life I was in over that three year period of time when I placed twice, I was not going to be able to be the parent they needed. I wasn't capable, at that time, to be their mother. I would have damaged them much further had I parented them. So I did the best I could with the circumstances I was faced with so they could have all of the opportunities I couldn't provide for them.

I was nineteen my first placement and twenty-one my second placement. By all standards, I was absolutely old enough to parent and could have done it. But I felt I wouldn't be enough by myself and I would hurt them more if they stayed with me. So my age may have had a maturity and financial factor, but ultimately I felt I wouldn't have been good for them to be raised by me in the dark seasons I found myself in.

We have always had a very open adoption, even though people were really uncomfortable with us being so open with each other that long ago, when open adoption was really just starting to become a bigger thing.

The worst thing anyone ever said about my adoption was asking if I would go back and get them back if I could, or if I would change my mind. That would mean having to decide between my current life with my husband and son PLUS my birth kids in our lives, or having parented my birth kids and probably never meet my husband or have my son. It's an awful question. I can't go back, and even if I did, it would be without the knowledge I have gained over the last eighteen years on my own adoption journey, so it basically would negate everything anyway.

But it's the best anytime someone validates my loss and sacrifice without making me feel like my kids are in a "better" place, or when someone says they have learned something through my story to help them or to help others be more ethical, empathetic and willing to educate themselves in their own adoption journeys.

To me, adoption means extreme love and tremendous grief, neither of which ever go away and often occur in the same breath. No one told me about trauma. No one told me about delayed grief. Women truly need to be informed about ALL OF THE THINGS that come with each option considered. We also need our own legal representation and deserve a lifetime of free post-placement care, support, and healing. We deserve help after the fact.

I encourage anyone looking into adoption to only work with agencies, lawyers and resource centers who truly offer genuine lifelong support post-placement for birth mothers. It is the ethical thing to do, to love us well even after we have placed our hearts with others - to not forget us and our role in adoption.

The biggest misconceptions I hear about birthmothers is that we are all on drugs, super young, have no support, and we aren't good people who don't love and then "give away" our children.

I wish people could understand that I chose placement because I truly thought my children wouldn't have all they needed if they stayed with me, that I would be damaging to them. And that I chose placement because I love them, even though it feels (and probably seems) extremely backward to love someone and let them go. But that is how I could show how much I loved them in that space, by giving them what I couldn't provide or offer at that time through two other people.

Love us well even after we have placed our hearts with others

I hate when people use the phrases "give away" or "gave up," because my children weren't old shoes that I unloaded to a secondhand store. They were deeply loved, incredibly wanted and that doesn't change because I chose placement. "Adoption rocks" is another hard phrase for me because, well, it doesn't. It's trauma and pain and loss then coupled with a couple or individual being able to raise a child, which can seem joyful and even beautiful, but the underlying foundation is a woman in crisis who thought separating herself from her child was "better" (another one I don't like) than her own ability to parent and provide. That's hard stuff.

Instead, I love anything that acknowledges one's loss along with another's gain. I love people willing to correctly educate on correct terms and phrases and language in adoption. I also love any inclusion of birth mothers and family in the adoptive family unit if that is possible and safe for the child.

The best part of my story is all of the love. We've had a lot of hurt, a lot of bad, we are in a really hard season currently, but the love is always there because we decided at the beginning of this to be a family and we have stuck to that, no matter how hard it is sometimes - because that's what family does. They have shown up for me and I have shown up for them. No matter where our story goes from here, I know the love will always be there.

Adoptive parents, never stop educating yourselves. For yourself, but especially for your kids. Their biology is super-important, never negate it or downplay it or make them feel badly for it. Embrace their cultures and ethnicities in tangible and mirrored ways in their lives. And lastly, never forget to love birth mothers/families well. They have sacrificed much for that child, so the least you can do is uphold promises made and love well, even in the hard times.

Adoptees, you deserve to be heard. We chose for most of you, you deserve to be given your voices back and to be truly listened to. Use your voices. Even if you are met with opposition, speak your truths. You are validated in what you feel about yourself and your story. Know that you are deeply loved and wanted, even if some of your family, adopted and/ or biological, may not be able to express that to you.

As a birth mother, I see you, I am listening. Find safe spaces where you will be understood and allow yourselves to process through your journeys. We need you, you are the voices of the education others need to hear, as you are the most affected. Keep speaking up. I am sending so much love to each of you.

SKYLAR

I am a forty-one-year-old mother of three kids that I parent with my husband of nineteen years. My first child was a son that I placed for adoption when I was nineteen. I was a college student living at home at the time I found out I was pregnant with him. The birth father wanted nothing to do with any part of it and so the entire weight and responsibility fell completely on me.

When my parents found out, they sent me to live in a maternity home where I was expected to leave without my son. They said if I couldn't marry the father, then it would be best for my baby

They sent me to live in a maternity home where I was expected to leave without my son.

and me if I placed him with a married couple who was older and stable. I was stunned and sickened at the thought of this and disagreed wholeheartedly, but with no support from my parents or the birth father and not knowing of any real resources for people in my situation, I went along with it.

So...I came home from there a completely different person with a whole new life, an empty-handed mother.

I never went back and finished my schooling. I've taken classes here and there and have had several odd jobs throughout the years, including some that I really loved. I've spent the last seventeen years caring for my kids that are my whole world, I've lived a pretty decent life, but somewhat going through the motions.

I've never taken any risks to do the things, career or school-wise that I always wanted to do, even when I had the chance. Honestly, I've pretty much kept to myself and not gotten too involved with anything or anyone. I've been in this sort of "holding pattern," just waiting for the day my son would become old enough to open the adoption and then everything would be right in my world again.

Of course, I know that's not realistic, but I guess that's what I told myself to get me through. I didn't even realize I had been doing this until just recently. He's now twenty-two and I'm still waiting for the day we meet, but I'm not holding my breath anymore, so to speak. I've taken big steps in processing what happened, I'm working on healing and I'm branching out and forming real relationships with people now. Things are starting to come together and it feels good.

The worst thing I've been told? "I could never give away my baby." That statement felt like a knife to the gut - the very last thing I wanted to do was give him away. And there is so much more to it than simply being pregnant, having your baby, and "giving it" to someone. It's clear to me now that people who say that just have no understanding of what it takes and what all you go through to place your child, but it still hurts to hear that.

My son's adoption is what's called semi-closed. To choose his parents, I looked through about a dozen albums of prospective adoptive families. When I made my final decision, I got to call them and introduce myself and tell them that I had chosen them, but we have never met in person. Communication began with sending letters and pictures back-and-forth through the adoption agency. When my son became an older teenager, we began emailing each other through the agency. My son's adoption was in Virginia, which means when he turned twenty-one, either one of us could legally request for the adoption to be opened.

I would have to say the best part of my adoption story is, without a doubt, the incredible life my son has had. That's all I wanted for him, and it turned out to be everything I could've hoped for. He grew up in a supportive, happy home with two of the most amazing parents I think I've ever seen. They've made so many of his hopes a reality. For example, at age five, he started begging his mom for piano lessons, so they signed him up and it turns out he is musically gifted! He writes his own music and frequently plays at his church.

He went to a Christian private school where he thrived, and onto a university, and now out into the world where he works for the family business. By all accounts, he has had a full and joyous life and is an accomplished, blessed and all-around good guy. I'm eternally grateful to his parents.

As a birth mom, what I would say to adoptees is this: over the years, I have met so many birth mothers online and in person, and in every case, no matter what the circumstances were, they put great thought and love into their decision to place. No one ever just "gave up" their baby.

And to adoptive parents I would say, please love us, the birth mothers. Please talk about us and acknowledge us. We just want to know you think about us, too.

TIA

My name is Tia and I'm thirty-five years old living in Oklahoma. I'm currently married with a son from a previous marriage and two stepchildren (ages fourteen, twelve, and twelve). We are expecting a little girl due early August. I work in healthcare analytics managing a team of analysts who handle a variety of reports and data for a local health system. I enjoy music and dancing (taught dance for twelve years at a local studio) and doing house projects and renovations as well.

I had just turned nineteen when I found out I was pregnant. I was at the end of my freshman year in college and had been dating the father for a few months. I knew right away I wasn't ready to get married and I wasn't ready to be a mom. I knew I would not be able to provide the life I would want him to have. So from day one, I knew that adoption was going to be the best thing for both of us.

A hundred percent yes, my age affected my decision to make an adoption plan. Like I said, I was nineteen. I wasn't in a long-term relationship to where marriage was something I could see for us. I was too young and immature to handle having a child and I wanted him to have more than I could give him.

They called my adoption "semi-open." I chose the family and met them three different times in person. After the adoption, I received pictures and letters every few months for the first year, and then every year for five years. After the fifth year, I have not had any more contact. I did send a letter at one point updating them on my life and letting them know I had another child which would be a half-sibling to my son who had been placed for adoption.

I wish people could understand that the process of placing for adoption was not simple. There was a lot of drama involved. I was a resident of Texas, but living in Oklahoma for school. The father had Indian (Native American) heritage, so if anyone is familiar with that, you will know that the tribes are not very willing to let their bloodline go. The tribe he was registered with contested our adoption decision and wanted us to choose one of their families.

We considered their parent profiles along with profiles from the adoption agency. When we did not choose one of their families, they made us go to court. This also meant that my son could not leave the hospital with his new family. He spent about ten days in transitional care. I then had to travel to Texas just so I could sign the papers relinquishing my rights in front of a judge.

At the time (at least, unsure if things have changed), that was not a normal process in Texas. I remember spending so much time crying over the fact that I just wanted him to have the family I chose for reasons I chose, and I hated that anyone would want to fight me on that. But in the end, it all worked out and he has spent his life with the family I knew he was meant to be with. God has a plan and he made it work.

The adoption day will forever be engrained in my memory as it was truly special. The day I signed my paperwork at the courthouse, I went straight over to the adoption agency afterwards. I was taken to a small room in which I got to spend some one-on-one time with my son. I gave him a bottle and just held him. I got to say my goodbyes in private.

Just because I think it was a wonderful experience doesn't mean I don't have struggles.

Then they walked me down a hall to another room where his adoptive parents, along with a couple of grandparents were waiting. My mother was with me as well. I got to hand him over to his new mom and we took a family picture. It will forever be one of the most special moments in my life. I knew he was going with the family he was meant to be with. Once I chose them, I started seeing so many commonalities between the two sides (birth parents and adoptive parents). I knew they were his parents.

To me, adoption means giving life to a child that might not have had one otherwise. You are giving someone a family they might not have been able to have, both for the adoptee and the adopting parents.

I can honestly say I can't recall ever having anyone say anything bad about adoption to my face. I think people often wondered how I was able to place my child. I think there are people out there that feel the child is better off with a biological parent, but I can honestly say I disagree. Sometimes I think that my thoughts are probably just as bad as what some people might say. Was I selfish because I wanted to finish college and do something with my life? I knew that would have been very difficult while raising a child. I wanted so much for the both of us, that I feel as if I was being selfish for us both and wanting to give us both the best life I could.

Most other positive comments are generally the same: "you were so strong," "you were so selfless," "you were so brave," "you did such a wonderful thing." Nothing was overly great to where I could say it was the best thing someone said. Everyone in my life at that time was extremely supportive.

I may make it seem like it was easy, but it's not. The decision was easy. Even handing him over to his new parents was not difficult for me. My mindset was such that I considered myself more of a surrogate. That was the best thing I could do to help myself deal with the situation. Even though I have never had any regrets, each year comes with different struggles. My son was born the day after Thanksgiving, so every year at that time, I get sad. I always miss him. I wonder what his personality is like, what his voice sounds like, how tall he is, and so on. I think about him daily. I can only hope that when he turns eighteen, he will choose to want to meet me, but there's no guarantee in that. There's no guarantee that I will ever develop any kind of relationship with him. Those unknowns are what make being a birth parent hard.

I think people misconceive that it's hard for me to talk about it and don't like to ask questions. That might be the case for some birth parents, but I am actually very open and love to share my story. I want people to know what a wonderful thing adoption has been in my life. But again, just because I think it was a wonderful experience doesn't mean I don't have struggles.

I think another misconception might be that people think the actual adoption process is the hardest time. Although it was hard and emotional, I feel like I've struggled with it the most once my life was stable, once I was married with kids and in a place where I know I could give him a good home and family. At that point, I found myself wishing I could have him back more so than in the first few years of his life.

I think being a birth parent is different for everyone. Birth parents with open adoptions will have misconceptions about birth parents with closed adoptions (and vice-versa). Everyone handles the situation differently. What I perceive as "normal" and true, might not be to other birth parents. So with that said, I think the biggest misconception is that a lot of people think that all adoptions are the same. And that all birth parents are the same because we all chose adoption... but that's just not the case. Every adoption is special and unique and everyone handles it differently.

PART TWO:

THE ADOPTIVE PARENTS

ALLISON

My name is Allison, and I am part of a Christian family from Texas. I am thirty-three, and I'm married to an amazing man and wonderful father to our children. We will celebrate fifteen years of marriage in July. We have two children. Our son (bio) is six years and our daughter (through adoption) is twenty-two months.

We discussed adoption before marriage and had decided that we would love to have children both biological and adopted. We wanted a larger family but that was just not in our story.

We went through a domestic private adoption that is technically closed but it's more like semi-open if that's a thing. I keep in

Love is what makes you family, not DNA.

contact with her bio uncle, and we are friends on social media. I thought it would be awkward but I love that we have a connection to that part of my daughter's life.

For me, adoption is a blessing and a chance to expand our family. We see adoption like our relationship with God, as in, we are adopted through Christ. Our approach with our child's story is honesty and openness. From the day our daughter was born, we have told her how much her bio mom loved her and wants the best for her, so she (bio mom) asked us to be her mommy, daddy, and bubba since she was unable to give the life she wanted for her. We speak of her bio mom often but refer to her as "Ms. Christie."

We wouldn't change anything about this decision. We want our children to know that adoption is a wonderful thing and how blessed we are to have her in our family. We also want to lessen any hurt feelings that we know can come up later.

People say all kinds of things about adoption. Best things: "I didn't even know she was adopted." "We are so blessed to have her in our family." "Guess what, Mommy? Sister is ours forever and nothing can change that."

Worst things: "She could almost pass for your daughter." I know it was meant to be nice, but she IS our daughter! "What happens when she wants to find her 'real' family?" We ARE her real family!

I want people to know that adoption's not all rainbows and butterflies. Sometimes it was hard and emotionally draining. It was hard waiting just because of the law about waiting six months, but we finalized when she was just over six months old, so it wasn't too bad. Every step of the way (and there were many steps), no matter what came up, God came through for us. When I look back, it was all worth it, and I'd do it a billion times over for her.

I wish people could understand that we love our daughter's birth mother. We pray for her constantly and hope that one day, she will be in a good place where she will desire a relationship with our daughter (when our daughter is an adult).

Some of the questions I hear include, "How did you find out about your daughter?" "What will you do if her bio mom tries to come into her life while she's still little?" And "How is it that your kids look so much alike?"

I hate the phrase "real mom/dad" when people are speaking of birth parents and the term "adopted daughter." Nope, she's not our adopted daughter; she's our daughter that happens to be ours through adoption. Also, "She's lucky you saved her." No, we didn't save her. We are blessed to be her family just as we are blessed to be our son's family. We didn't adopt her to "save her." We wanted to be her family and with that comes keeping her as safe as we can and loving her as best we can. No child needs to just be safe. They need love.

On the other hand, I'll always agree when people say, "You are so blessed," or "What a beautiful family."

To adoptees: you are not our adopted children. You are our children that happen to be ours through adoption. We love you just as if we shared DNA. Love is what makes you family, not DNA. To birth parents, thank you for choosing life.

Thank you for choosing to allow us to be a family. You are not a failure. You are brave. You are loved beyond words.

AMELIA

My husband and I had been married for twenty-five years. He had a son from a previous marriage, so in the beginning, we decided not to have children.

I am a nurse and years ago, I was working one night with a boy who had been dipped in hot water. He had third degree burns to both feet, multiple bruises and adult bite marks all over him. He was fourteen months old and had recently been adopted from Ethiopia. He rarely cried and when he did cry, it was more of a whimper; he was listless and wouldn't look me in the eye or eat. He was absolutely beautiful with huge eyes, and I fell in love with him and made it my goal to get a smile out of him before he left.

When his mother came in the room, he would turn away from her. I took him for X-rays and a CT scan of his entire body. His mother didn't even ask if she could go with him. He was in our hospital for several weeks and never had toys brought in from home or a favorite blanket.

I knew enough about the laws in our state to know that her rights would be terminated. We started the foster care process with the hopes of eventually adopting him. We sped through the application and home inspection as fast as we could. We proceeded with the foster process, got certified and eventually her rights were terminated, and from three prospective families, we were chosen to adopt him. We had a room all ready for him, clothes, toys.

The day we went to the social services office to meet him and start the transition to our home, a sister of the adoptive mother decided that she would take him as her eleventh child. We were devastated.

I finally was able to come to a place of gratitude for the time I did have with him. I am his prayer mom, and I still pray for him to this day and I pray that one day God will be gracious to let me see him again.

After we recovered from that heartbreak, I began to wonder if maybe God had a different child in mind and if putting the love in my heart for that child had opened my heart up to adoption. I knew the agency he had been adopted from and before long, we were on a list waiting for a boy.

I read every adoption book I could get my hands on while we waited for him to come home. Like most children who come home after being in an orphanage, when he fell and got hurt, he did not come crying to me for comfort - that didn't come for probably a year or more. The Sunday school teachers couldn't believe he would hit a kid or grab a toy and show absolutely no remorse for having hurt another child.

He hoarded food, which is not uncommon for children who are food-deprived. Once, I was talking with the bank teller and someone said, "Ma'am is that your child?" I turned to see him digging through the garbage looking for food. I began to carry a snack in my purse, food for him anytime he wanted it. He only ate it a couple of times but knowing it was there was enough to keep him from digging in the garbage. He had his own food drawer in the kitchen where he could keep all the packaged food he wanted - his drawer and his alone. He still has the drawer, though eventually he stopped keeping food in it and today it's filled with loose change, sunglasses and odds and ends.

I joined a couple different adoption groups mainly for support. I soon found out people on those sites didn't want to talk about any real issues. I wondered if I should take him to a counselor to help with attachment, but I didn't know where to go or who to turn to. I would ask questions on the sites and was quickly told not to talk about things like that because it might scare other people from wanting to adopt.

I asked around until I found someone who recommended a counselor and we made an appointment. There were times when he would just sit in a trance-like state, his eyes glazed over staring off into space. I now know it's called *dissociation*, a common sympathetic nervous system reaction to trauma. We hear often about fight or flight, but there is one more response not often mentioned: freeze or dissociate.

This expert in counseling told me when my son dissociates, I should tell him he is doing that because his birth parents died and that was a very traumatic thing. Looking back now, I can't believe I actually did what she told me to do. But she was the expert, so I figured she knew what he needed. One day he looked at me and said, "I know my parents died - why do you keep reminding me every day?" Ah, the wisdom of a six-year-old who actually knew more than the expert! He was right; I wouldn't want to be reminded of that every day either, so why was I stupid enough to actually do it to him? We didn't go back to that counselor after that.

Then I met a social worker who was also an adoptive parent. She was learning a special type of therapy targeted specifically at improving bonding. We began seeing her and soon I saw some amazing results in relation to his dissociation and attachment to me. But he still struggled in school. I requested he be tested and he was found to have a learning disability and ADHD.

While all this was going on, my husband and I decided to adopt again. I called the same agency and told them we were interested in a boy around eight or nine years old. Our first adoption had taken seven months from beginning to having him in my arms; this new adoption would take two years.

It wasn't too long after when I received a phone call and was told about one young boy who had been at a different orphanage and all the other children had been adopted except him - he was the last one. He was transferred to our agency and we began the process of adopting him.

I continued to look at pictures. Another precious little face kept popping up in all the pictures. I would see the picture of his sweet face in my sleep, and I would hear the words "a boy who needs the love of a mother."

I called to learn more and my heart broke when the voice on the other end of the phone told me he had no family waiting. Her exact words were, "No one wants the boys, especially the older boys, they're very difficult to adopt out." He had come to the orphanage the same day my first son left. He was a little younger than the boy we were in the process of bringing home. For the next week, I could not sleep, and those words "no one wants the boys" kept going through my head. Then I would hear another voice saying, "God wants boys."

For the next two weeks, I argued and wrestled with God. We couldn't afford three children. There was no way! I had pictures of the boy we were adopting and I loved him; he was my son and I couldn't wait to bring him home. But I finally gave in...we would bring both boys home.

My sister and I flew to Ethiopia to pick them up while my husband stayed home with our first son since school had just started. The night before I met them, I had so much anxiety: What had I done to my family? What was I doing? What was I thinking? I stayed up reading the Bible, searching for and praying for words of encouragement.

There really aren't words to describe how you feel that first day you finally get to hold a child whose picture you have fallen in love with. It's surreal! The boys didn't speak English, but we had fun driving around the city, spending a few days getting to know each other. I don't think they were told they were going to be adopted or maybe they didn't really understand what that meant.

That began what would turn out to be a couple of really difficult years with our oldest[1]. I had an Ethiopian friend come over and talk to him several times to try and figure out what was going on, why he was so defiant and angry. He said no one asked him if he wanted to be adopted, no one asked him if this was what he wanted.

It took me a long time to really understand, to see things through his eyes. Imagine living in the only place you have ever known and suddenly you are taken across the world to a strange place with people you don't know. Halfway around the world, no one looks like you, the food is not familiar, you

---

[1] Author's Note: Amelia's oldest son was not the first son adopted.

have no idea where you are or what would happen if these new people leave you. What would you do? How would you react? That would be a very scary thing to happen to any adult with good coping skills. But for a child with no coping skills and lots of anxiety...it spells disaster.

I had read probably two dozen books on adoption: books on transracial adoption, adopting traumatized children, adopting older children. And most of the really important stuff I didn't learn from any of these books. It was "on the job" training. I guess I never thought about the fact that something that made me so happy and was so wonderful in my eyes was really a horrible tragedy in their eyes. The worst thing that could ever happen to a child has happened to them - they've lost their parents. For them, adoption began with pain, sorrow, and loss whereas adoption for me began with love, happiness, and excitement. So right off the bat, we start out on two different pages.

Many people think adopted children will be thankful and grateful to now have a family and a home. When in reality, there is nothing for them to be thankful or grateful for. They've lost their family, culture, national identity and language. They've lost so many things. They had no choice - no one asked them if they wanted this. What they had may not have been wonderful in the world's eyes, but it was all they knew, all they had, and they didn't know any different. Gratitude is a learned behavior, even for adopted children.

Temper tantrums in a two-year-old is one thing, but a temper tantrum in a nine-year-old is a totally different thing. Especially a nine-year-old that doesn't speak your language. No book told me what to do during a full-blown temper tantrum at 35,000 feet in an airplane. Or a screaming, yelling, flailing temper tantrum in a crowded restaurant. Or a screaming fit at midnight in a hotel in another state where you're worried that the police would be called and you'll be hauled off to jail. So, I read more books and thought to myself what I really needed was a book called "How To Hug a Porcupine."

The feeling of isolation was above all the worst. I finally stopped talking to others because they just didn't understand.

Many of the books I read had a common theme: *love is not enough*. That really confused me because the Bible teaches all you need is love. "Love endures all things, hopes all things, endures all things." So I began to try to understand what all these authors meant by "love is not enough." And if love is not enough, what else did I need?

The feeling of isolation was above all the worst. I finally stopped talking to others because they just didn't understand. "Yeah, your kids have screaming fits and your kids are difficult to deal with at times," I thought to myself, "but it is *not* the same." It wasn't their fault, they just really didn't understand, and I learned I couldn't talk to other parents about our situation.

No, we couldn't go anywhere or get a break. Our saving grace was the few friends we did have that had adopted children and totally understood. I think one of the most important things in adopting older kids is surrounding yourself with supportive people who understand - other adoptive parents.

In addition to supportive people who understand is a strong faith in God. One day, while reading the Bible, I came across 1 John 4:18 which says, *"There is no fear in love. But perfect love drives out fear, because fear has to do with punishment. The one who fears is not made perfect in love."* It was then that I realized it had been here all along and I knew it.

The experts were wrong again: without love, you have nothing. I'm sure my son was afraid - who wouldn't be? It's love that drives out fear. The house falls without a firm foundation and that foundation must be love. I had to love him before things could ever change. The more I read the Bible during that time, God showed me that love is not a feeling - love is a commitment. I could not love him on my own, God had to love him *through* me.

About the time, I was finishing a book that was actually pretty helpful. It wasn't a book on me helping my child to change, it was a book helping *me* to change.

When children are out of control and have no coping skills, they look to adults to teach them how to cope with their emotions. When adults react to the child's emotions with anger, indifference, or the same emotions, kids become more out of control. The child looks to the adult to be calm, to know that even if they feel out of control, there is someone in control. To be effective, adults must teach the children how to deal with their emotions by responding and not reacting. My son's wild emotions were pushing my buttons, and I was *reacting* instead of *responding* to him. So the problem wasn't my son - the problem was me.

I'm not saying my son didn't have any issues we needed to deal with - I'm saying the way I was dealing with them was making them worse. At this rate, if I continued with what I was doing, then we were headed to an unhappy place for all of us.

We needed a game plan, we had to do something. We decided to pick one behavior and work on that one behavior. Each day, we would try a different approach, and each night, we discussed what worked and what didn't and made a new plan for the next day. We tried a different method until we found the approach that worked for that behavior, then went to the next behavior until it was under control. In addition, when I tucked him in bed each night, I would kiss him on the head and tell him I loved him and I would say one thing that he had done well that day. Some days, it was all I could do to say, "You did a great job brushing your teeth today."

I began watching him closely for his triggers - what happened right before the wild emotions? I soon realized he was triggered by change. I took almost everything out of his room and made it so he only had to make simple decisions - only a few clothes, a few toys. And always talking about what to expect and what was going to happen.

His behaviors slowly began to change. One night, after kissing his head and telling him he had been a rockstar at getting dressed that day, he smiled at me. That big, toothy grin made me cry, and I knew right then we had won!

Not long after all this, I spoke with an author writing a magazine article about the difficulty some adopted families go through. In the article, I said I hated my oldest son. I cringed at this - how would I be judged? But it was the truth at that difficult time, it was how I felt, and I wanted our story to help other families who might be in the thick of it as I was.

I figured my kids wouldn't read a women's magazine, but what I didn't think about was that several mothers whose children attended their school would. It didn't help that what I thought would be a small family photo at the end of the article turned out to be a two-page centerfold - kind of hard to miss a picture that big.

I thought I was safe as time passed, until about a year after the article was published, my son read the article and came to me with the book in hand. "You hate me?" he yelled. We had a long discussion, and I reminded him about how difficult our first years had been.

I said, "You hated me, I could see it in your eyes." He admitted he did hate me. I told him I thought for a long time I did hate him, but I realized now that love is not a feeling - it is a commitment. I would never give up on him; he was my son and would always be my son.

A friend of mine, one of my supports and an adoptive mother of five, said from the beginning that my oldest would one day be my best kid. And she was right - I could not be prouder of the young man he has become. He is a joy, funny, and dependable. He moved out this past year to go to college. He understands his anxiety about change and has worked through most of it. He is traveling by himself to universities out of state, scouting where he might attend in the future. We Skype and text several times a week - I miss having him home.

Before my youngest came home, I had the story of how he came to the orphanage and a few photos from an author who wrote about the HIV crisis in Ethiopia. We placed a picture of him with his birth father on his new headboard. The day he came home, he recognized his dad the first time he saw it. He took the book to school for show and tell for several years. When he was eight or nine, he would ask me to read his story to him from the book. I would hold him and we both would cry.

My older boys have wonderful memories of their mothers. I guess I should stop here and explain my feelings on these adoption terms. I totally understand that "birth parents" is the politically correct term to use and that many adoptive families are offended by the term *real* parents or just *parents*. But each adoption situation is different.

They were loving parents - you can see that they loved their children, and I know that my children loved their mothers and fathers. My oldest two have wonderful memories of their parents. We call them "mom and dad" - and they call us "mom and dad." My kids never question which mom or which dad we are talking about.

One of my coworkers, who is an adoptive mother, explained to me after I referred to one of my son's mother as *mother*, that she feels "mother" is a special term that is only used for one very special person in one's life. I have to say I totally agree with her. In Ethiopia, the kids called everyone at the orphanage "mom" - the laundry woman, the cook, the woman who ran the orphanage were all "mom" or "emaye." That's why my boys had no problem calling me "mom" from the moment they met me, but I don't think it had any meaning to them.

In Ethiopia, names have a great meaning. Mothers who carefully chose such wonderful names for their sons whom they loved so much can't, in my opinion, be reduced to just biology. My coworker was right. The word *mother* has very special meaning - how could I call these amazing women anything but mother? I don't feel that demeans me or lessens my importance in any way. I am their mother now; she was their mother then.

Last year, I contacted an agency that locates families in Ethiopia. The day we left Ethiopia, both boys had aunts and uncles at their goodbye party. We sent pictures and letters to each family and received short videos, several pictures and a letter from their families. It will be harder to locate extended family for my youngest since we have so little family information. We hope to one day return to Ethiopia and visit family we can find.

All the books and experts say, "Don't adopt out of birth order;" none I found explain why. I found out why on my own. When you adopt a child younger than the age of your current children, that child is not only younger in age, but will regress in age and be younger emotionally. Also, my oldest son was very jealous of my youngest and became abusive toward him. I could NEVER leave them alone together. It was like having an infant all over again. It was probably a good thing that my youngest was from an orphanage - he was a fighter and no one pushed him around because he fought back.

I love my kids and wouldn't change a thing from my end, but I am not sure how I feel about international adoption from the child's perspective. Is adoption really the best thing for them? Taking them from their culture, language, food, people? The tremendous difficulty my oldest went through in the beginning, and my middle son has struggled with survivor's guilt. He has struggled with his identity and wonders whose characteristics he has. His teen years were extremely difficult and there were many times he told me I was not his *real* mother. It crushed me to hear those words spoken from that cute, smiling face I fell in love with from the pictures. It makes me wonder if there is another option, maybe helping support them in their home country?

Sometimes people say strange things, but I don't get offended by their words. I truly think they don't know much about adoption and are curious. If you are not a part of the adoption community, you wouldn't know the language, and I don't think we should expect them to know it. I didn't know it until I started to research adoption. So, it makes no sense to me why some adoptive parents are offended when people ask what happened to their kids' "*real*" parents." It's an opportunity to teach others the term "birth parents," no reason to be offended.

I think people are just curious and don't mean anything by it. A woman in the grocery store once asked me how much my son cost. I think she looked at me and my son, who is obviously not my biological son, and thought, "Isn't adoption really expensive? She doesn't look rich." I explained there are different costs along the way for fingerprints, court filing fees, agency fees and travel expenses - but no matter the financial cost, my son is priceless.

I think, by far, the most difficult question people ask is what happened to my boys' parents. If I do answer the question honestly and say their parents died, the next question is always, "From what? From HIV? Do your boys have HIV?" So most of the time I just say, "We don't know."

Also, it just makes me feel uncomfortable when people say things like, "You are a really good person for doing that," or "I could never love someone else's kid." I don't think anyone goes into adoption because they feel they are really good people or trying to prove something. Rather, you choose adoption because you want to love a child, you want to have a family. I don't see them as "someone else's kids," because they are *my* kids.

Something I do really hate is school projects like "my life timeline" or "my family tree" or better yet, "bring in a baby picture of you." I know there are all kinds of creative ways to do these projects (birth parents as the roots of the tree, etcetera), but the issues we had were not really with how to do the project, but more of the feelings the project brings up. My kids didn't want to answer all the questions when these projects were on display in the hallway. Kids just want to be like everyone else, they don't want to be different or stand out.

I don't think the school thinks about how these projects cause kids to relive very difficult times in their lives. Not all kids are prepared to handle those difficult questions, nor do they all have the coping skills to work through those difficult things and feelings in front of the world.

I think adoption is a beautiful story, a mirror of our relationship and adoption into the family of God. In the beginning, my boys didn't really understand what it meant to be in a family. They didn't speak our language, didn't know our customs, routines, or how everything worked. Adoption is not easy, but with God on our side, we made it through! I can't imagine how hard it has been for my boys, and we are so proud of them. In the end, I realized if I had ever found the book I was looking for ("How To Hug a Porcupine"), I would have found that *I* am the porcupine.

BETHANY

My name is Bethany. I am a wife and a mother of three. I am a business owner as well as a Department Manager for another company. I have been married for twenty-eight years and my children are fifteen, seventeen, and nineteen. From a very young age, I knew I wanted to be a mom. I wanted that before any profession or education. After three years of marriage, finishing my Bachelor's degree, and getting a little work experience under my belt, my husband and I decided to start our family. After nine years of marriage and no children, I was very frustrated.

We discussed In-Vitro Fertilization and adoption. I think the final decision to move forward with adoption was because we didn't want to spend the money on IVF for a *maybe* pregnancy. If we adopted a baby, we paid when the baby is placed. We didn't care if the child was our biological child or not.

My husband and I originally chose to go through our church social services department, mainly because the cost was much less than other options. After months of preparations and paperwork, and being on the waiting list in the state where we lived, we were given a career opportunity that sent us to another state. When we moved to the other state, there was a much larger wait list and it would take much longer to adopt. We decided to look into private adoption agencies at that time and chose one in our area. After only a few months, we were matched with a six-month-old African-American boy that was in foster care.

I never felt any difference in love between my adopted kids or my biological child.

My children have never not known that they were adopted. We brought up adoption right away, and I wouldn't change anything about the way my kids found out they were adopted. As soon as my kids knew what "being pregnant" meant, we talked about them being babies and growing in another mommy's tummy (both of my adopted children had the same birth mother). We talked about birth mom a lot. We wondered what she looked like and what her favorite food was, favorite sport, etcetera. I took every opportunity to let my kids know how much I loved her and that I hope to meet her one day and thank her for giving me my family.

There have been good and bad comments made. Both of my adopted kids are black and the best and worst experiences were with people of color. The worst experience I had was when I was in the Los Angeles Airport. As I was walking through the airport, there were a lot of eyes on me. Black women stopped everything they were doing, tapped their neighbors and all eyes were on me - and not one smile. Nothing was *said*, but it was very uncomfortable.

The best experience I had was a UPS delivery man who came to my home for a delivery. He saw my son who was a toddler at the time and smiled at him. The UPS driver started to walk back to his truck but turned around and came back to my door and said, "Thank you for your part in bridging the gap in society! It really makes a difference."

I want others to know that I never felt any difference in love between my adopted kids or my biological child. Adoption means a Mother's LOVE. It is the love of a mother who puts their child's needs first and allows another mother to meet those needs. Adoption is the ultimate sacrifice a mother could make. I felt the tug of that sacrifice after I was finally able to conceive and I gave birth to a child. My adopted children were four and two when I gave birth to my biological son.

Funny little story: my adopted kids joke and say they are more special than my biological son. They say to our youngest son, "Mom and Dad chose us, and they had no choice with you. They are stuck with you."

We do not have any contact with biological relatives. I wish that people had more compassion for my children's birth mother. I get so upset when people make comments like, "How could someone give up their own child. That is so selfish and irresponsible!" I have also had people negatively respond that she "gave up" two of her kids but kept the one in between them, or they will say how selfish it was of her to keep that other child.

I always get asked why my children's birth parents made an adoption plan and they say, "Why did she do it?" I wish people could understand that we don't know what Birth Mom was going through in her life and, in my opinion, she is the most selfless person in my life and I have never even met her. I will never judge her for her decision and my love for her increases every day as I parent *our* children.

The best part of my family's adoption story is that I have two full-biological adopted children and that their birth mom requested that my second child be with her brother who was two years old at the time. She wanted them to have each other.

CHARLOTTE & MASON

Mason and I live in Cedar Park, Texas, a suburb of Austin. We love to travel, hike, fish, and go camping. I am a pediatric cancer survivor which limited our ability to conceive naturally. I also learned that I carry a deadly genetic syndrome, and I was told at a young age that I may not be able to have children. I also struggle with endometriosis and lost an ovary and my uterus during my first surgery to remove a benign cyst. We knew that we wanted a family and felt adoption was the best choice for us.

We went through an open domestic adoption. Lily was six months old when everything was finalized. The fear that we had about losing her melted away. It's been a wonderful experience knowing her birth family.

We are still working on how to tell our daughter Lily about her story since she is two and her language is developing. She will always know she is adopted. We don't hide it and she sees our birth families regularly. We send them pictures and we are all friends on social media. It's a great way to keep in touch.

Lily has known her biological family since the day she was born and we see the birth mom and her family often. She knows that she has a Mommy (Charlotte), Daddy (Mason), Tay-Tay (Lily's "nickname" for her bio mother), Chip (Lily's bio father), Grandma (Mason's mom), Grandpa (Mason's dad), Grammy (my mom), Nanny (my stepmom), Gramps (my dad), Me-Maw (Lily's bio grandmother) and Granny (Lily's bio grandmother on Chip's side). Lily also has aunts, uncles, and cousins from all of our families that she knows too.

We weave conversations about her adoption in our everyday conversations. For example, when we watched Disney's *Lilo and Stitch*, I told her that Stitch was adopted. Then I told her that she is adopted, too.

She hasn't asked any questions yet. We expect that there will be many and we are trying to be prepared to answer them. I wrote a lot of stuff down in her first year of life, feeling fearful that we wouldn't see her biological parents again. That isn't the case and the last two years have shown us that we are one big extended family.

In the back of my mind, I always wonder if the biological family thinks we are doing a good job or is happy with the amount of time they get to spend with Lily. One day, I received a thank you note from Lily's bio-grandmother where she wrote that we were great parents. It was the peace of mind that I needed and the reassurance that we are navigating parenthood and open adoption in a positive way.

Expressions I hate?

Number One: When Lily has a meltdown or challenges our role as parents, people who know that she is adopted (especially older folks) will say, "Remember, you asked for this!"

This is so aggravating as I don't think they would say that to someone who naturally gave birth.

Number Two: "She doesn't smile in pictures. We were worried that she wasn't adjusting to adoption well."

Huh? Wow. Just wow.

Number Three: "I couldn't have an open relationship with the birth family like you guys. I don't know how you do it."

I hate this one the most because our birth family is probably less dysfunctional than many other biologically-related families. The birth family is really great! Sometimes we pinch ourselves at how great they are. The myths about open adoption are real even today and the struggle is real to overcome bad perceptions about open adoption.

To me, adoption means, "an act of love." Also, adoption is not for the faint of heart. Like when I meet people who are trying to conceive and they say, "If we can't get pregnant, we'll

In the back of my mind, I always wonder if the biological family thinks we are doing a good job.

just adopt." It's not so simple to *"just adopt."* I used to say that all the time. Silly me.

Each adoption agency is different. Each birth family is different. Each process is different and the heartache behind the scenes is real. I think eighty percent of matches don't go through.

Our first expectant mom decided to parent because the father decided not to sign away his rights and forced the mother to parent. It was a domestic violence situation and just sad to watch. At the end of the day, the situation worked out and it wasn't meant to be for us.

The grief was awful for us. We never really rebounded and then dealt with our adoption agency being slow to match us again. That's a long story in itself, but we struggled with our adoption agency and didn't always see eye-to-eye with their ways of handling our adoption.

There are still questions we always get asked:

"Are you going to go through adoption again?" No.

"Are you ever worried that she will be taken away?" Not anymore.

"Do you think she looks like her birth mom or dad?" Does it matter?

Phrases that I hate:

"I have no news this week." When we got this from our adoption agency.

"Just be patient, your time will come." This was when we were in limbo when we were waiting for a match.

"Isn't adoption expensive?"

My favorite phrases: "I love you, Mommy!" "I love you, Daddy!"

Each story is different. There is no rule book. There is a lot of information out on social media, the internet, and in book stores. A lot of it is helpful. We learn as we go and we are also taking it one day at a time. I tell others, "Be prepared to know that it's not as rosy as some adoption agencies like to promote. It's a very weird, emotionally-charged and soul-searching experience."

For us, it worked out the way it was supposed to. Our entire family grew in love, in people, and in joy with Lily's arrival. She has impacted so many of us in a very positive and loving way.

CHRISTA

Author Note: Christa Jordan opted to use her real name since she is also an author and did not share any info she has not already shared in other mediums. She can be found on Instagram @spoonfulofjordanblog

I am a wife, stay-at-home mom, and writer. We are a homeschool family and currently have one child through adoption (five-year-old boy), and hope to grow our family again through adoption.

My husband and I are both believers and followers of Christ, and we believe that Scripture is clear that we are to "learn to do good; seek justice, correct oppression; bring justice to the fatherless, plead the widow's cause." (Isaiah 1:17) To us, adoption is not only bringing children into your family, but also fighting against unjust systems, advocating for those who don't have a voice and helping to preserve first families when possible, and stepping into the brokenness. We don't believe that every believer is called or meant to adopt or foster, but we do believe Scripture is clear that social justice is mandatory and that can look many different ways! For us, that does mean adopting children into *our* family, but serving and educating in many other ways as well.

We adopted internationally from Japan, and it is a closed adoption. Our process was very different in that we had an agency here who helped us with all the initial paperwork (conducted home study, initial immigration paperwork for non-Hague convention countries, everything that needed to be done in order to receive USCIS approval to adopt internationally), but we were responsible for finding an agency in Japan for child placement. There was not an existing program like most agencies have in-country, so we essentially took on a private international adoption because adopting from Japan is so rare.

Once we found an ethical agency in-country to work with us, we worked with them personally to do all the necessary paperwork the Japanese government needed. We were matched with our son when he was four months old, traveled six weeks later to obtain his visa and receive guardianship rights, and brought him home at five months old. Our agency here in the US completed all the post-adoption services, sent necessary reports and paperwork the Japanese government needed, and we finalized when he was eleven months old. Soon after, we began the naturalization process for him and finally received his citizenship when he was two years old.

We chose adoption to grow our family because that is the way we were led. We have no fertility issues, we simply believe this is the way we meant to grow our family. It's something we are both passionate about and, honestly, what drew us to one another. We both have backgrounds in social work and experience working in child welfare. For me personally, I just always felt like I was supposed to be mom to those whose first moms, for whatever reason, could not take care of them. Not in a "rescuer" or "savior" kind of way - I believe that kind of motivation can be very damaging. More so in a "I'll stand with you" kind of way. I just knew I was meant to share my motherhood because my heart is not only for these kids, it is for their birth families too.

We have been open and honest about our son's adoption from the very beginning, even before he could talk or "understand." When he was preverbal or just starting to talk, we simply found ways to weave it into conversations and celebrate it. For instance, if we saw an airplane in the sky and he would point to it, we would say something like, "Yes, that's an airplane! When Mommy and Daddy adopted you, we flew to Japan, and then we flew home together as a family!"

We would talk about his birth country, show pictures, and consistently pray for his birth mom. As he got a little older, we would share his story in the most simple, age-appropriate ways, like, "Your birth mom carried you in her tummy, and you were born in Japan. She wasn't able to take care of you, so she made a plan for you to be adopted. Mommy and Daddy wanted to adopt, so we adopted you!" Obviously that has grown into deeper, harder conversations with more of his story revealed as needed and as is age-appropriate, but we've always had the policy of openness and honesty from day one, making it a normal part of our family conversations, because that is how our family came together!

It's obvious he was adopted since we are white and he is Japanese, and celebrating his race, ethnicity and birth culture has also been a part of conversations and woven into our family. I wouldn't change anything about our open and honest policy. Hard conversations have come much sooner than I imagined, but I wouldn't change that. People around me - some family and close friends - have tried to tell us that part of our struggle with him processing everything is our fault, like we've done it too soon and someone so young just can't handle this kind of information. I have had to let things like that roll off my back, even though it's hurtful and sometimes I feel a pang of doubt like, *are they right?* But when I listen to adult adoptees, I know that we are doing the right thing.

The only thing I would really change is I wish I would have changed some of the language we used in the beginning, things like "gotcha day" and even "forever family." But at the same time, that's even opened up beautiful conversations for us to have to go back to him and say, "Hey buddy, we're not going to say that anymore. Your birth mom will always be your birth mom, so saying 'forever family' isn't fair." Admitting that we are still learning and growing, we're going to make mistakes, but we are willing to apologize and change things for the better, listen to him, and I pray it goes far deeper than we know.

To me, adoption means *family, fully and completely*. It is full of complexities, loss and gain, joy and pain, messy and beautiful all at the same time. But at the end of the day, despite it all, we are family, no matter what. My son is my son, not my adopted son, he is *my son,* fully and completely, and just because I didn't give birth to him makes me no less his mom. I don't know what giving birth is like, but I do know how much I love my son, and I would go to the ends of the earth and do all of this ten times over if that's what it took.

I wish people would not see adoption only as an alternative if you are unable to bear children. Adoption has always been plan A for us, never plan B, because there is more than one way to build a family, and our family is no less valid simply because we do not share DNA. It doesn't make his birth family invalid either. No one needs to be diminished, because the most beautiful thing about adoption is there is room enough. True love always makes room, therefore there is room enough for all of us.

Honestly, I think the best thing is just people acknowledg-ing that we *are* a family, without a tagline or two cents of what they think about adoption. So when someone asks if we adopted our son and we just simply say yes, a response of, "That's so awesome!" or "What a beautiful family!" is all that's necessary. Just acknowledging that we are a family, and we are real, with no intrusive questions is the best thing someone can say. Or I love meeting other adoptees! Sometimes, someone will ask, and they'll then tell me they were adopted, and it's just this instant connection and sweet conversation. I value that so much.

Sadly, I could fill this page with many more negative things that people have said than positive. Worst thing, I have a few: When we were in our adoption process, we had some friends who once introduced us to someone else by saying, "They're kidnapping a kid from Japan basically." We were very young and the first in our "friend group" to grow our family this way, so I know that comment came from ignorance, but it was so hurtful and this is the kind of ignorance that perpetuates awful stereotypes about adoption. We had to fundraise in order to cover the full cost of our adoption, and we definitely had a few strangers on the internet tell us we were kidnapping or child traffickers. It was awful.

I've had people say some really racist things, like, "At least he'll be able to pronounce his L's and R's correctly," and other things, especially about immigrants. The worst now is when people ask extremely personal questions in front of him, asking about his biological family or the automatic assumption that he was abandoned and how awful it is that any mother would do that. The worst thing said in front of him has been, "So how much did he cost?" I corrected this question, but there was a very difficult conversation with loads of questions the next couple of days from my son.

The biggest thing I want people to know about adoption is that it is very different from your experience as a biological parent. It doesn't make one harder than the other necessarily, but this is the loneliest road I have ever walked. Parenting a child who has endured trauma is the hardest thing I've ever done, even though I wouldn't trade being a parent in this way at all. There is *so much* I cannot share that goes on in my home, things that we are dealing with that people just don't know, and I cannot share it without violating my son's privacy and story, which I just won't do. And who would want their struggles blasted everywhere for the sake of understanding? It wouldn't be fair, but truly, unless you've walked this road, you have *no* idea what dealing with all the complexities and emotions and trauma adoption brings is like, so please don't compare your parenting to mine like we are dealing with the same things.

No one could have prepared me for the loneliness and lack of community of this part of my motherhood, or the *shame.* I constantly feel misunderstood, people jump to assumptions, and I have never been so judged before I became a mom in this way. Again, it's all worth it, but it's the hardest road I've ever walked.

I'll never forget him looking around the courtroom, probably wondering *what in the world is going on, why are these people here staring at us?* It was both the greatest day in the world and one with such deep loss. I was so, so thankful he finally, officially had our last name, this sigh of relief that we could finally just focus on being a family without the constant paperwork, phone calls, trips to the mail, and visits from social workers. It was one of the sweetest moments to finally be declared his parents, to finally hear his full name called out. But also the gravity of that moment, it's hard to put into words looking into his eyes, knowing he is mine, yet knowing he was hers first, and we've never even met. There was so much to take in, so many emotions, but overwhelming love and thankfulness. Much like the day I first laid eyes on my beautiful boy, I'll never forget it.

We don't have a relationship with any of the birth family and that has been really hard to navigate. There are so many questions he has that I can't answer, and I wish I could just pick up a phone or send a message and ask. But that's not our story. If it were possible, we would totally be open and willing to have those relationships, and I hope they are able to reconnect one day. I would love to meet them too.

I wish that people could understand that you are not going to know or understand everything, and that is okay!

You don't have to have all the personal information to accept the fact that we are 100% a family, but there are things that are different and complex for us. The fact that yes, adoption is amazing and beautiful, but it also begins with loss, and there is no way around that, and that is going to have an impact for the rest of our son's life and our family's story. There were so many amazing things that only God could do to protect our son's birth mom, him, and bring us together as a family. That is not lost on us, and adoption is just one way we see redemption in this world, but you can't have redemption without brokenness.

The best part of our adoption story is that God literally made a way where there was no way. I fell in love with Japan as a teenager but never dreamed that I would have a child from there. About a year before we officially started the adoption process, we knew international adoption was going to be what was best for our family in that season, but we didn't just want to pick a country where we fit the requirements, we wanted to be intentional.

Japan was just it for me and made sense. I had never heard of anyone adopting from there and did research for a year. It was possible, but in the grand scheme of things, just barely, and *far* from easy. Only about thirty adoptions were approved each *year* in that country at that time.

There were so many odds stacked against us, but we knew without a doubt this was what we were supposed to do.

People thought we were crazy, and there were so many times I thought it was going to fail. But we continued to just put one foot in front of the other where He told us to, and if I could tell you how it all aligned, well, you would see that He made a way where there seemed to be no way. It was deliberate, intentional, crazy, beautiful, scary, long and winding, but the best part is how we were brought together, three strangers turned family. The moment I laid eyes on my son, I knew what love at first sight meant.

The power of our love for one another is greater than our brokenness.

I always get asked:
- "Are you his mom?"
- "Is he adopted?"
- "Where's his *real* mom?"
- "I'm shocked you got a boy!"

That phrase "real mom" - I loathe it. It completely invalidates my motherhood, it communicates to my child that I'm basically just a placeholder, that my love isn't the same for him and our family isn't a true family. It communicates to birth mothers that there is only room enough for one of us to be important, and I think deepens the guilt and shame that she had to place her child in the first place. It's an *awful* phrase.

I also hate the phrase "own children" as in, "Do you think you'll ever have your own kids?" or, "We'll adopt when we're done having our own kids." Once again, a little louder for the people in the back, you do not have to give birth for them to be *yours*. Pregnancy and childbirth is *one way* to grow your family. It is not *the way*. If they share your last name, they are yours, end of story. When you say things like this, it communicates to the adoptee that they don't really belong, which of course, is one of their greatest fears. My son is my son, adoption is simply the way he came into our family.

Adoptees and adoptive parents: *We need one another.* We need your voices, we need your perspectives, we need your relationships. We are on the same team, despite what so many would say, and if we remember that and can listen to each other, work together, then we are definitely better together. I know that so much has been stolen from you in the past, and I long for your healing, I long for that to be restored. I am *for you,* I stand with you, and the power of our love for one another is greater than our brokenness.

DANIELLE & FORD

Author Note: These are the adoptive parents of Russell from my book Through Adopted Eyes.

We didn't get married until we were thirty-eight and forty-three, so at the time, we both had careers and wanted to enjoy being married for a while before having kids. By the time we decided, God had decided something else. I was too old and even if I could have gotten pregnant, I would not have been able to go through nine months. A sad time. We thought about adoption but it didn't really seem like something that feasible. So years went by.

A friend of mine from up north also could not get pregnant and decided to do some research into Russian adoptions. One day in 1999, she called me and asked if we would be interested in adoption from Russia. Huh? My friend had done all the research on an adoption agency on the east coast that worked with Russia.

My father had passed away six months prior and he had left us some money, so this adoption seemed possible. I lost my mom, sister, and my dad all within five years. So having something/someone of mine was very important. We got the paperwork from the agency. There was tons of it... But they guided us through it and we completed the paperwork by December of 1999.

Once the paperwork was finished, the agency sent us a one-minute video of our future son Russell. OMG, the minute we saw him, we said, "This is it!" A big smile across his face and big blue eyes... My husband and I have brown hair and brown eyes, but he was adorable. He had holes in his clothes, no diaper, it was a pathetic sight. The agency told us that he was really small even for a child in an orphanage. Russell weighed fourteen pounds and he was sixteen months old!

In the video, his hands were clenched and our home study lady said that could be a sign of *spina bifida*. So we sent the

It is amazing how you can love someone you have never met.

video of Russell off to the University of Minnesota who, at the time, was doing a lot of research on kids adopted from Russia. They said the same thing: "Spina bifida." Scary. So we had a doctor in Moscow that was trained in the West go visit Russell and tell us what he thought. More scary news: Russell was in the hospital for chicken pox; the doctor said he just looked small and hoped he would make it…

But there was something about that precious face and that smile - we said we wanted him. From that moment, he was ours and all we wanted to do was get him out! It is amazing how you can love someone you have never met. More paperwork, but in April of 2000, we went to Moscow to go get Russell.

He was actually in an orphanage in a town about three hours from Moscow. Our agency had set up for us to live with a couple in Moscow who would take us where we needed to go, feed us, and they were familiar with the adoption process. You really need someone who is familiar, because there is so much to know, who to give gifts to, and we had to go over to Moscow with $8000 in cash that we kept in a money belt, and a box of all kinds of things for the orphanage. It was not cheap to adopt, of course, but the money is so secondary.

It was a little scary when we got to Moscow. New big city in a new country. There were policemen on the streets with guns, which was a new sight for us. It was stressful. We were so stressed out that we did not see many sights, instead we elected to drive by the Red Square which was still exciting. We also found a huge McDonalds and we ate there almost every meal because it was nice to have something familiar.

We did get to stay in our own Russian apartment for a night and it was very nice and made the experience a lot less frightening. The next morning, we got to finally go to the orphanage where we would meet Russell for the first time in person. They took us to this room, which was kind of dreary, and they told us to wait. The rest of the orphanage was not for guests.

They brought out Russell, put him on the floor and asked, "Do you want him?" I thought, *Is this happening?* When we saw this precious face, we said, "Of course we want him." All of the cute clothes we brought him were too big because he was only fourteen pounds but we managed. The orphanage staff was very kind and they said that they loved Russell and told us that he was always so happy and they held him a lot.

We left the orphanage with Russell and went to the courthouse for the adoption. It was kind of frightening to be in a Russian courthouse. We were nervous because, by Russian standards, we were too old to adopt a baby, but with Russell being small and sick, they approved us.

We took Russell outside and then realized he had never been outside. He didn't know what grass was. The small things were so exciting for him. He didn't talk, walk, and hadn't eaten much. But our hosts made up for that with a huge bowl of mashed potatoes with all kinds of vegetables in it. He ate like he had never eaten before and it felt like we had gotten past that hurdle.

We didn't get any information about his birth family, but when we got him, we were just happy to have him. We knew we would not have any problems arise related to open adoptions. But now with all the ancestry things, I do not know if he could find anything out about his family. Russell does not seem to be interested in any DNA tests except he told us he wants to know who he looks like. I think we have the same mannerisms. People do not realize he is adopted.

We had a big party when we got home from Russia. We took him to the doctor, we had a few surgeries, but he is healthy now. Russell is now a Junior in college with a goal of becoming a biomedical engineer. He is the best child, and we are so lucky to have him in our lives. We have never had issues with bonding and we always told him he was adopted.

Adoption is not a scary word to him. He is still smiling and has a wonderful temperament.

The worst and best thing people say is, "Oh, you are such wonderful people for adopting..." No. While it was our pleasure, we just love him, but that does not make us better people for adopting.

One other thing...my dad's birthday was in December and he also passed away in December of 1998, the same month Russell was born. It just seemed like it was meant to be.

I would tell anyone to take a leap of faith and bring a child home. It will be the best thing for both of you...no doubt about it!

ELIZABETH

My name is Elizabeth, and I was born with two heart conditions and have had four open heart surgeries. I'm not very close with my parents and didn't have a great childhood. I have a BS in Political Science and traveled the world on a program called Semester at Sea. I paid my own way through college and am debt-free. I married my high school sweetheart and I have a great home, job, and two kiddos. I'm extremely passionate about financial education, adoption advocacy/education, and travel.

We struggled with infertility for a year, I had my heart surgeries to consider, and we are carriers of cystic fibrosis. We decided to not start infertility treatments of any kind and decided to focus on adoption. We just wanted to be parents. We really didn't understand the whole process and implications when we first started.

Both of our kiddos were adopted domestically. We have relationships with the birth family. My daughter's birth mom and I are very close and talk weekly if not more. Originally, it was closed but then I started to talk to her directly against agency/attorney advice. I have a relationship with my son's birth parents but it's not as strong (granted he's only three months old) and there is still healing needed. We attended his twenty-one-week ultrasound, too. We all hung out in the NICU after his birth and took photos together. I talk to his bio-grandma often. We are all friends on social media. The experience is just like any relationship - it takes work and has a lot of love in it.

For me, adoption means "beauty from brokenness." I wish it wasn't needed and hope to see the adoption process drastically change. I feel incredibly lucky to parent my kiddos. It really has made me the person I am today. I've learned so much and continue to do so. I've gained an even bigger extended family through it.

Please know that the heart aches. There is a roller coaster of emotions. The lack of control. The costs. Not all adoptions are the same. Every story is different (which makes it even more difficult to explain to people).

My daughter is almost four but there was no big moment of telling her she was adopted. She's always known. We have kid adoption books, I made her a book myself, she's FaceTimed with her birth mom, and we talk about it very openly. Obviously, as she gets older the questions will become more complex. My son is three months old right now, but he will always know too.

It amazes me how often people ask us if our children know or will know of their adoption. I always want to respond, *"Why would I tell the world/family/friends and not my kid? Like I expect everyone to keep a secret?"*

The worst thing someone has said is about the focus on my child's looks/race. I hate the assumption their birth mothers are young or drug addicts. Or the assumption that my children must have issues from the assumed birthmother's drinking/drug use. People also assume that we picked them out of a catalog. SO MANY misconceptions.

I also hate when we are made to feel like martyrs or told how lucky our kids are. The guilt I feel, mom guilt, guilt for adopting...just so much guilt.

We have heard good things, too. "I love your family," or "I can see the love you have for each other." "You are lucky to parent those kids and you all have a beautiful family."

I want people to know about the corruption that occurs. The expenses. The difference between domestic adoption and foster care. Many don't understand foster care is run through the government and that domestic is through private agencies/companies, etcetera. There are not many regulations on domestic adoption through a private agency, no required unbiased counseling or legal assistance for the expecting family, etcetera. Also, people don't understand foster care is a temporary home and the goal is to *reunify* the birth family or reunify with other kin.

It is frustrating when adoptive couples feel that they are owed a child.

My daughter was ten days old and my son will probably be about four months old at finalization. We don't really celebrate the finalization date. I hate the word "gotcha day" because we were there when they were born or immediately afterwards. Although it's a day we dressed nice and took a picture, we don't have it framed or hanging up. That day symbolizes us legally becoming their parents but also the loss of their first family. I also like to think we were there for them before that date, so what does it matter?

The best part of our adoptive parent story is that we were matched/selected early on in the pregnancies for both and had time to really dream and bond. Both kiddos had NICU stays and one had a med flight trip (obviously not best, but now looking back it's what makes our story ours). How everything lined up, how we met or matched with the birth parents, there is so much that needed to happen. I love the openness we have with our birth families. Oddly, I feel like this was meant to be. I don't mean my kiddos were meant to lose their biological family, but that I was meant to be their mom. I was meant to adopt to help advocate and to be open about all of this.

We get asked a lot:

- Why the birth parents "gave up" their kids.
- What was the cost?
- Not understanding difference between domestic adoption and foster care.
- What race my child is… *insert eye roll*
- People incorrectly say that our kids are lucky… Um, no *we* are the lucky ones.
- I love when people say: beauty and brokenness of adoption.
- Favorite quote: "A child born to another woman calls me mom. The depth of the tragedy and the

146

magnitude of the privilege are not lost on me." (Jody Landers)

I do not like when people use the term "birth mom" before the baby is born. She isn't a birth mom, she is an expectant mother, and might choose to parent. It is frustrating when failed adoptions or adoptive couples feel that they are *owed* a child when really, it should be celebrated that the birth parent decided to parent.

To adoptees and birth parents, I want to say that not all adoptive parents are bad. Most just don't understand the process or your perspective because we weren't told about it. Companies and agencies gloss over and sugarcoat a lot. Movies/TV make adoption seem only like rainbows. I'm trying and learning every day. I continue and hope to see more adoptee and birth parent perspectives.

JENNIFER

Hello, I'm Jennifer! I'm thirty years old and live in Ohio with my amazing husband Samuel and our gorgeous daughter. I am very close to my family. I love to read! Bookworm is an understatement.

I have always wanted to adopt. For some reason, I always pictured myself adopting internationally. Samuel and I thought that we would adopt AND have biological children. Getting pregnant isn't in the cards for us, though, and that's okay!

When Samuel and I decided to start pursuing adoption, we did a lot of research. A lot. We looked into many adoption agencies, and the cost was astronomical. Looking into foster care seemed like a logical next step. The paperwork was identical to some of the agencies we spoke with but the cost of adoption was much less (free). In that moment, we began to question the cost of private adoptions and decided to move forward with foster care. Did you know there are about 400,000 children in foster care in the United States, and that more than 100,000 of them are waiting to be adopted? Wow.

We love being foster parents. We have loved five children unconditionally. Our very first placement was an adoptive placement, which is very rare. In foster care, children are removed from their birth parents due to abuse, neglect, or abandonment. The goal of foster care is always reunification, but sometimes it's just not possible. Our adoption is thankfully open (which is usually not the case with foster care).

Our beautiful daughter was ten months old when we met her. Samuel and I began sharing her adoption story with her immediately. After finalizing her adoption, I created a photo book for her. It reads like a fairytale and explains how she came to our family. She loves books, and I felt like this was an age-appropriate way to start introducing her story with photos of the people in it. Samuel and I talk about her birth family and adoption often (she is now almost three).

We finalized our daughter's adoption when she was eighteen months old. I think her age was bittersweet, because she was too young to understand the impact of what was happening.

Adoption means so many different things to me. It's so complex and always changing. Adoption means family and brokenness. It means pain and love. Adoption means trauma and healing. My family was built from brokenness. What an amazingly, terrible truth that is.

The best thing someone has said to us about adoption is how lucky my husband and I are to have our daughter. Which is so unbelievably true. The worst thing that has been said to us about adoption is how lucky our daughter is to have us...

I want others to know that my adoptive parent experience is always evolving. I'm continuously learning from all sides of the adoption triad. No two experiences are the same. Many people think you adopt and that's it. This couldn't be further from the truth. As adopt-

I wish more people understood how important it is for an adoptee to know where they came from.

ive parents, Samuel and I are always learning more for ourselves and educating others about adoption where we can.

Our family has a great relationship with our daughter's birth mom and siblings. When adopting through foster care, this usually isn't safe (children are removed from the home with good reason). Because of this, Samuel and I took the relationship at a snail's pace. Our daughter's safety will ALWAYS come first, but we also know how important the relationship with birth family is (when safe and possible). Our daughter loves her brothers and sisters so much! It's amazing seeing them together. We really enjoy learning about our daughter's birth family and supporting her birth mom.

I wish that people understood that people can change. The majority assume that our daughter's birth mom is horrible and that we shouldn't have contact with her. People make mistakes. All of us. I wish more people understood how important it is for an adoptee to know where they came from.

The best part of our adoption story is - hands down - our daughter. She has taught us so much about love and life. Man, we are so lucky!

Samuel and I get a lot of stares and inappropriate questions because we adopted trans-racially. We just smile and educate where we can (while guarding our daughter's story). I am a firm believer that you don't know what you don't know!

I hate when people ask, "Oh, well where are her real parents?" I kindly say, "We are her parents. Are you asking about her birth parents?" Sometimes I simply say, "We are her real parents," and watch the confusion on their face before walking away!

As foster parents, Samuel and I also hear a lot about how "bad" foster kids are and how we should be careful letting them into our homes. It's very frustrating! Kids aren't in foster care because of something *they* did, but because of something their parents did.

Adoptees and birth parents: Please keep sharing your truths! As an adoptive parent, I learn so much from you. You are important, valued, and loved! Thank you for educating me and so many others!

KALEB & DEMI

I'm forty-three, a business owner, and have a large extended family...not sure what else you would want to know. We went through the Foster to Adopt program at our agency.

We found out after a couple of IVF trials that Demi would most likely not be able to get pregnant. After some soul searching and talking with friends and family, we came to the conclusion that there are a large number of kids that are without a good family and we could provide one.

The route we took, fostering to adopt, was gut-wrenching at times. We fostered our first foster son from a couple months of age right up until his first birthday, when the court allowed his mother to get him back. This made very little sense to anyone involved - CASA, attorneys, and so on - but it didn't seem to matter to the court.

It's best to investigate and talk with multiple families and agencies.

We almost gave up on the whole idea but decided to try once more. We ended up with another foster child who had no birth parents in the mix that we ultimately adopted. It wasn't long until we got the call that our first foster son, now two years old, was back "in the system." When they picked him up, he was wearing a diaper that was at least a week old and searching under a couch for his bottle. Thankfully, we got him back.

He was returned to us saying fewer words than when he left a year prior. Ironically, looking back, as painful as the process was, we wouldn't change the outcome for anything. Had we not lost him for a bit, we may never have ended up with both.

We stressed out nonstop about how to tell our children their stories. We read different recommended approaches. Finally, we planned on telling them once they were both six, thinking they might understand then. A classmate beat us to it, telling them they were adopted before we could. They didn't have a clue what that meant, though.

So we started with a couple of children's books to explain adoption and use it as a stepping stone into the conversation. They either didn't follow or didn't care at the moment we read to them. Now we reinforce the concept by bringing it up in conversation: "Did you know So-and-So is adopted, too," etcetera. Still not sure they understand, but at least they are hearing it and not afraid to discuss it.

I'm not really sure what we would change about this, besides beating the classmate to telling them. Maybe bringing it up earlier, although they don't seem to understand now, so I'm not sure that would have mattered.

With our first son, we kept a very open line of communication with his mother and very briefly with the father. When we went to court to try to get our first foster back, the father's family tried to protest it. By keeping the dialogue going with the mother, she ultimately convinced the father and testified on our behalf that he should remain with us. Without that, I don't think we could have gotten him back. With our second, we have a great relationship with his aunt, uncle, and cousins - they've become part of our family.

The thing I wish people could understand about our story is that it's not unlike many others. In the end, you must be selfless and focus on what is best for the needs of the child or children. Have a close support system of friends and family in place to pick you up when feeling let down by a troublesome system.

When they were little, we would get asked, "Are they twins?" They are six months apart but resemble twins abut as much as in the *Twins* movie with Schwarzenegger and DeVito - very opposite! When we would answer, "No, they are six months apart," you could see the calculation start in their mind...pretty funny.

"What was it like?" is another common question. And if we get into the story, it's usually one that can turn off a potential foster/adoptive parent, so we are careful to explain how our situation could be much different from someone else's and it's best to investigate and talk with multiple families and agencies if considering adoption.

A client of mine told me the best thing about adoption: "I was adopted, and I'm thankful every day for it." The worst I've heard from many people: "I gave up because the process was either too painful or too cumbersome."

I hate the following phrases and words: "the system," "the court," "the process." But we love hearing: "Mommy, Daddy," because the best part of our story has been ending it with two amazing little boys.

To adoptees: I can't say for sure without having been through it myself, but I can imagine there will be a lot of questions from our two about whether or not they were "loved" having been available for adoption. I think their parents/families made the biggest sacrifice they can, giving them to a loving family knowing they may not have been able to provide for them themselves.

Birth parents: Do what is best for the child, no matter what. If you don't think you can provide for yourself and the future of the child, then it's your responsibility, having brought them into the world, to find someone who can.

Adoption means providing someone the chance of an upbringing in a loving household. For us, it means being a parent to two great boys where we otherwise may not have been able to.

KENDALL

My name is Kendall. We have adopted twice. We were told that we should not conceive due to health concerns. We wanted children and researched surrogacy and domestic infant adoption. We felt that infant adoption was best for us.

For our first adoption, we used a domestic adoption agency. We initially had a semi-open adoption with our daughter's birth mother but now have an open adoption. We used a consultant for domestic adoption and were matched with an agency for our second adoption. We have an open adoption with his birth parents.

My children were both infants when we adopted them. Our daughter was seven months old and our son was three months old. I can't really say that their ages at finalization impacted us in any way.

Our son is two, so we have not started the specific discussion of his adoption yet. With our daughter, it was a very organic process. She has always been an emotionally mature and inquisitive child. I am an adoption social worker, so adoption is a constant conversation in our home. As she asks questions, we answer them in the most honest way we can, while honoring her birth mother. There are some things we feel she is not mature enough to hear at the moment, but have always strived to answer questions and provide the information she wanted and needed in an age-appropriate manner.

We have always talked about adoption with our children. Our daughter became very curious and needed more information as we were going through the adoption process with our son. There were a lot of conversations around this time when she was five. These conversations and her desire to know more about her birth mother are what led us to pursue an open adoption with her - this had originally been semi-open.

Adoption often comes from a place of brokenness for the birth parents *and* adoptive parents. I think that should be acknowledged. I don't think that most birth parents "want" to place their children. There are often life circumstances that lead birth parents to adoption.

For some adoptive parents there has been infertility, infant loss, or other life circumstance that brings them to adoption. The statement "beauty from brokenness" always comes to mind for me. Adoption can be a beautiful process. Adoption is the way my husband and I became parents, so we will forever be grateful to our children's birth parents for their bravery and selflessness in choosing us to be their parents. There's no way we can ever thank them enough.

I want others to know that the process requires faith - a LOT of it. Your faith has to be strong enough to overcome any fears you experience. I also want others to know that open adoption is not scary.

We did not know my daughter's birth family prior to placement, but now we have a relationship with her birth grandmother, birth sister, and aunt. Our relationship with her birth grandmother allowed us to reach out to her birth mother when we wanted to pursue a more open relationship with her. It was very helpful and we are glad that we had a way to reach our daughter's birth mother, that we would not have otherwise had, when our daughter needed to forge a relationship with her.

It's amazing to have found my true calling through our adoption journey.

When it comes to phrases I hear, "what is her real name" or "who are her real parents" are really the ones that seem extremely insensitive. But I think that I feel well understood regarding adoption.

Of course THE BEST part of everything is that I get to be Mommy to two amazing children. However, through adoption, I found my passion. After the birth of our daughter, I felt very led to work in the adoption profession. I started working with adoptive families about three months after she was born and now, almost eight years later, work full time with adoptive parents and birth parents. It's amazing to have found my true calling through our adoption journey.

I have a unique perspective on things as an adoptive parent and adoption social worker, so I have many opportunities to educate people about adoption. I get asked lots and lots and lots of questions, but I love to share my experience with families!

Adoptees, know your identity, seek information about your birth family, ask your adoptive parents to be a part of that with you. Identity is so important to our children! Birth parents, don't be ashamed that you made an adoption plan for your child. Acknowledge your worth, your selflessness, your brave decision....but also acknowledge your grief, your loss, and seek support from other birth moms, counselors, support systems. Know that you are strong and amazing.

LEIGHA

My name is Leigha. I am thirty-five years young and am an elementary school teacher in California. I have been married to my high school sweetheart for over eleven years now. We have three amazing kids and love to travel in our RV as much as we can.

Adoption chose us. I never, ever say it was "our backup plan," though. They were the best "yes" we have ever spoken! I have always had adoption influences in my life, especially through my teen years and I always felt the Lord leading me that way.

I also felt the Lord preparing me at a young age with the notion that I would never carry a child within me but, at the same time, always having the strong desire to be a mother. He started preparing my heart for this, so after a few years and a few procedures and roadblocks, I mentioned the idea to my husband, and the rest is history. My husband has a laundry list of medical problems and he always says how thankful he is that he didn't pass that down to a child.

My kids are a six-year-old son, three-year-old daughter, and two-year-old daughter. They are my life and my pride and joy. Our kiddos are all adopted through foster care. However, my son is also a surrender and my girls are biological sisters.

We have had some contact with our daughters' birth mother through court-ordered visits as well as an older sibling of theirs that came into foster care after our youngest daughter was born. My girls have a large number of siblings but we have only been able to contact the one of them.

My sister was able to foster their sister while her father went through the reunification process. She was with my sister for over a year and a half, which was amazing and such a blessing, and I wish they were older so they would remember her.

My son, being a surrender, we have no contact and no records at this time with any birth family. At this age, he has no desire to even talk about the subject of his birth mother, but I bring it up every few weeks so he knows we are here when he is ready.

My children have always known (to age-appropriate degrees) that they are adopted. It has never been a secret and always celebrated in our home and family. I have learned that, without bio family contact, the concept of adoption is so very hard for them to grasp at these young ages.

That being said, we use lots of books as avenues to talk about it. We also pray for their birth families every night as a way to keep them in mind and help our kids learn that they will always be supported (when ready) to explore and search for relatives if they should choose to.

Adoption means family to us. Literally and physically. Adoption means brokenness but stability. It means love of this one and his/her birth family. It means God delivered you into our hearts and He is always your first and true Father above all else. It means a forever journey of loss followed by an equal journey of support and love from us and our Lord.

I am not easily offended by any remarks or comments about my kids or their stories. I don't take offense to the naive or blinded view of adoption others may have.

Also, my kids are still really young and don't really stand out as being adopted so we don't get that many strange, off-the-wall comments or questions or turn many heads. And if we do, our kids are young enough to not be too affected by them. My kids were all within three months (plus or minus) of their first birthday when they were adopted. So their very young age made the finalization process easy and very uncomplicated for them and us.

My favorite comments are when people come to me inquiring about how to foster and help our community through foster care because they have heard our story.

I think the uniqueness of each and every story is huge. I also know I share more about my kids' stories than some. However, I feel that each and every one of their stories, about how they came to be ours, is so incredibly tied to an absolutely amazing God who wrote and scripted every single detail. It truly is awe-inspiring and just solidifies how amazing and powerful our God truly is.

I also don't think some outside of the adoption triad (or even some within) have considered what a tough road these kiddos will have as adoptees. I know when I started this process myself, I was incredibly naive to this thought.

We always get asked if the girls are twins, which they aren't. But they do have the same birthday! Our daughters are exactly one year apart. Our oldest daughter was born and we never once saw her birth mother. Not in court and not for visits. Nothing.

Our youngest daughter was born and we figured it would be the same story. However, this was not the case. When their older sister came into care one week after our youngest was born and also had visits, then birth mom attempted to show up for visits as well as to court. The interactions with their mother were stressful and at times unsafe. She was not mentally stable and viewed us as the people "taking her baby," as if we had stolen her. She would sometimes be aggressive toward us as well. She seemed bitter at the situation and made us feel like it was our fault somehow.

The three months that visits lasted were some of the most stressful days of my life. This tiny baby of mine was put through these visits when really - in my opinion - she only wanted to see the older child. Their sister would do most of the caring for my daughter at visits. It was a really hard environment to try and establish any sort of relationship or connection with her like I wish we could have.

As mentioned above, we had the girls' half-sister (now eight years old) for a blessed one and a half years. Unfortunately, we do not currently have any contact with her, however, we

I also don't think some have considered what a tough road these kiddos will have as adoptees.

made it clear she would always be welcome to find us and see her sisters as long as she was making good choices in her life.

I think, for foster parents in general, the loss of a child is the hardest part for others to understand. The "how could you do that" is always the one we get. We do it because we were called to serve and love *"the least of these."*

People have also asked, *"How could you give the older sister back?"* I didn't want to but I love her and my kids enough to do what is best for them.

Some have asked, *"How do you deal with everyone (department employees) all up in your personal space and life?"* Well, I don't like it, but it's worth it in the end. Oh, and I have nothing to hide.

I love the phrases:

- •"Born in our hearts"
- •"Adoption is love"
- •The quote about "the depth of the privilege and magnitude of this loss not being lost on me."
- •"One less orphan"
- •So many Scriptures that point to all of us being adopted by God or about adoption in general

Adoptees: Cherish the family you have today. There is nothing wrong with looking or being curious (we fully support that), but at the end of the day, the family members who God has put in front of you that day should be a blessing (bio and/or adopted). Having a thankful heart, in all aspects of life, is what God wants us to have. Each of you are an incredible blessing to your families - two families in fact! Let the truths of the Lord guide you in all you do!

Birth parents: No matter what, establish some sort of way you can communicate with your child and them with you when the time comes (email, PO Box, etcetera) even if you want a closed adoption. Also, it's not all about what you want. That child may need or want to know you some day and leaving that line of communication open could be vital to their wellbeing.

The best part is God. He is the reason each of them are mine. The story He wrote for each of them blows my mind every single time I think about it. And for each, it is all about timing! God's amazing and PERFECT timing for them to enter the world and our family. Again, only a story He could write!

LENA

From the very first few dates, my husband and I talked about how we were interested in being foster parents. We both have a strong desire to help others and better society. We both knew having a family would be very important to us and we decided to get married young to start a family.

After three painful years of infertility, we decided to switch up our plans and start fostering. We went into foster care in hopes to adopt a child. We were warned of the pain and uncertainty foster care brings to everyone's lives. But it was the only way for us to be a mom and dad. We thought, even if we only have a child for a day, we would be helping that child. And so we adopted our two sons, Chris and Dustin, out of foster care.

All adoptions in our state (Pennsylvania) are considered open, but adoptive parents get to decide to what extent we allow biological family members in. Chris and Dustin are not biologically related so they have two separate cases. Dustin's biological mother was in the middle of court cases where the state was going to terminate her rights when she eventually agreed to sign over her rights. Chris's biological mother's rights were terminated by the state. In both cases, the biological mothers were not happy to be losing their children and resented my husband and I.

Even if we only have a child for a day, we would be helping that child.

Our sons are two and three years old. They don't remember their adoption days and can't grasp the concept quite yet. We have large photos hung in our living room of the boys on their adoption day holding a sign. We are very proud of those days and we hope to celebrate their "adopt-iversary" every year!

We plan to raise both boys knowing they were adopted and how special we are to have been placed together. I want the boys to grow up knowing that they are adopted and that we fought for them. I tried saving everything from that period of time to best explain to the boys about foster care and adoption. I want to have an open relationship with my children and be able to answer the questions that are on their minds.

Dustin was seven weeks old when we picked him up from the hospital. He was placed in the foster care system at birth when he was born with five substances in his system. He was in the NICU for seven weeks, going through withdrawal. We were chosen for him by his caseworker. Out of all the other wonderful foster families, we were CHOSEN for him.

Chris was an emergency foster placement. We were lucky to have been able to answer the call for him that night. Though the road was full of ups and downs, we made it through foster care to his adoption.

For me, adoption means that they are wanted. The older stigma of adoption is that children were unwanted or unloved. But to us, adoption means we fought to have these little boys in our homes forever! Their adoption brought the fighting to an end and was a start of our new lives as a family - without caseworkers, lawyers, judges and advocates. We had to report EVERYTHING to these people and were never allowed to make decisions for our children without their consent. It was freeing to enroll my child in preschool or take him to the doctor without reporting to someone else. And we were constantly battling with the biological mothers because they tried to keep as much control over their sons as possible. The adoption meant that we had all control over their lives and we could raise them as we saw fit.

Chris was two and Dustin was nineteen months old. Dustin only knew us and his adoption day was fun! Chris, though, was scared of all the added attention. He wouldn't sit with us at the bench. All he wanted was to lay in the middle of the courtroom with his face hidden. It was a very Chris thing for him to do!

We have a "handshake" agreement with the biological mothers to keep in contact. We agreed to up to four visits a year and they both have my phone number. They are always getting new phone numbers, so I let them come to me if they want updates. This past spring was hard because Dustin's mom relapsed. We had a date to meet her at a local park on Saturday and Friday we had an unexpected visit from CYF (Children, Youth, and Families Office).

They had to investigate our family because his bio mom was ChildLine.[2] She does not have custody of any of her own children but has Dustin's older sister often. CYF was investigating us to make sure we didn't adopt Dustin and then give him back to her. I guess it's a common thing? We were mortified they thought that but as soon as the case worker came in and saw Dustin attached to me and the huge

---

[2] ChildLine is a division of Pennsylvania's Department of Human Services responsible for accepting reports of suspected child abuse.

adoption day photo on the wall, she dropped her attitude and became more compassionate to us. Once we found out about the relapse, we canceled the visit and then never heard from her. We worry about Dustin's bio sister, but it is out of our control.

Chris's biological mother is battling multiple terminal illnesses. We hear from her every few months. He has a handful of older siblings. They have been interested in getting to know Chris but that's a lot for us to take on. Chris's older brother was adopted at birth to a nice family in Ohio. I recently came in contact with his adoptive mom and we are now close. We hope to raise the boys to have each other as a support system.

I get annoyed when people say, "They look like you," or "the boys aren't biologically related? They look like brothers." I am proud of how they entered our family and if they look like us, then that's completely a coincidence.

I get asked a lot if the boys have any medical conditions from the drug use they were exposed to. Chris appears to be fine but he was born three months early so he was in the NICU for an extended period of time. Doctors are very impressed with Chris's health. Dustin is very small for his age. He has been monitored by Endocrinology for his height and weight. They think he will need growth hormones eventually. They believe he is so small due to the smoking and alcohol he was exposed to *en utero*. Dustin was also recently prescribed glasses. He struggled with a lazy eye when he was an infant and now this has reoccurred with his farsightedness. They believe it's related to the exposure as well.

I hope people understand the fight we had to adopt these boys and that even though the adoption is finalized, it's not over! We still have to occasionally deal with CYF and their biological families. We live in the same city as them, so eventually we will run into them.

Chris and Dustin sharing our last name and forever with us is the best part of our story! It was a great day when we received their new birth certificates with our names on them! I want others to know how rewarding the experience of foster to adopt is. When we think about the lives our sons might have had if this all didn't take place, I get anxious. These little boys brought so much love into our lives.

I love when people ask me about their journey and how they can become foster parents too. I share our family's story because I want other people to open their hearts and homes to children in need. Even if it's just for a few nights, we are helping these kids.

LILI

My name is Lili, I am an adoptee, and as of this year, an adoptive mama. My birth mother was sixteen when she had my birth sister and eighteen when she gave birth to me. She worked with my adoptive mom (who I just call *Mom* but I know that can get confusing when explaining). My parents tried to conceive for over thirteen years, and they had adopted two children before me. My birth mother told me she felt as though she was pregnant with me for my mother, and always knew she was meant to raise me.

My parents adopted five children and ended up having two biological children after. I have never felt different from my siblings, oftentimes I forget I'm adopted. They are truly my best friends. I have always, always known I was adopted.

The word *adoption* to me is extremely beautiful, messy, and hard all in one. It's very complex. It's life-giving and loving, but comes from brokenness.

I have wanted to adopt since I was a little girl. That's what built my family and I always thought it was so special. When I met my husband, we spoke about adoption and how growing a family would look for us.

To me, I was always called to adopt first and if the Lord also wanted to bless us with biological children, that would be great too. But something has always triggered me my whole life when I heard, "We couldn't have our own children, so we adopted," or "We are devastated we can't conceive, so we are going to adopt." Like adoption is the next best thing. I understand there is infertility and adoption is such a beautiful way to grow your family; we just need to work on how we word things and how it comes across to the adoptee.

Anyways, my husband and I were married one year and decided it was time to adopt. I did a lot of reaching out and research on where and how we wanted to do this. All my adoptive siblings and myself were adopted through the foster system, my mom got a call about my brother when he was born at the hospital and his mother decided parenting wasn't the best choice for her, and my mom went and brought him home that day. The rest of my siblings were a little older - around three years. We really wanted an infant because I was adopted as an infant and I always liked how my mother chose to place me instead of the state taking children away and finding homes.

I did have a closed adoption, but I was able to meet my birth mother and birth sister when I was eighteen. I waited until I was twenty-one; I didn't have a need to meet them, I mostly wanted to know what they looked like. I felt like there was supposed to be this crazy bond and reuniting would be emotional. But to me, they were just strangers. Over the years, I have tried to be in my birth sister's life, but sometimes

I forget because I have my family and we are all so close and connected, and it doesn't come natural for me with my birth family.

When I was twenty-five, I started asking my birth mother for more info, like if she knew who my birth father was, etcetera. She didn't like that and blocked me on everything, so to this day, that is a closed door and she is no longer reachable. Having this rejection happen to me as an adult hurt worse than I ever thought possible. There were times when I was figuring out who I was in the typical middle school age range, and I would beg my mom to let me contact my birth mother. Looking back now, I'm sooo glad she didn't; I couldn't imagine going through this rejection as a preteen.

I definitely think there are healthy open adoptions and I see them all the time. I also thank God my mother protected me from that all these years. Plus, my birth mother is bipolar and not regulated by a doctor, and to have her in my life then, out on an emotional roller coaster, would have been stressful on me as a child. I have never worried about my mental health or thought anything of it until I met my birth mother.

When you adopt, you become that child's parent - you have to do what's best for your family and child's interest. Every circumstance is so different. So, I see healthy open adoptions and lots of people pushing and hoping for them, but sometimes it's not the healthiest choice.

Never promise a birth mother something you aren't comfortable with or planning on following through with. I'm so grateful that God led my birth mother to my family when she didn't see parenting as an option. She had an abortion appointment but cancelled it and chose to give me life. Someone once told me more than half of pregnancies are unplanned, but there are no unplanned adoptions; I've been loved, chosen, wanted before I was ever born. My parents have loved me so well - I have a great life. Both my parents did everything they could to make sure I was happy, healthy, and loved.

It's important to know where you came from...and what makes you, you.

Foster to adopt is a great way to grow your family and I encourage it. But for my husband and I, we decided to go with domestic infant adoption. We signed on with an adoption consultant group to help us navigate the process. Washington state is not an adoption-friendly state and it's very hard to get info, and there's around 2-5 adoption agencies all with extremely long waiting lists to even sign on with them. We got our home study done within two months in September, and in November we were matched with my son's birth mother, and by December he was in our arms.

Ben will always know he is adopted. He is four months old and I already tell him his adoption story and about his birth mother. I figure if I start now it will hopefully just be natural and easier to talk about when he's older. I have pictures of his birth mother when she was pregnant with him, and health history, and his original birth certificate. When we were in the town he was born in (his birth mother's home town), we took pictures at the hospital, beaches, and his birth mother and family. I've made a baby box full of things that he can keep and have. It's important to know where you came from and your family history and what makes you, *you*. My husband and I will always be honest with him and tell him anything he wants to know.

When the birth mother relinquished her rights, it was actually to the agency, and the agency gave us temporary custody. We have had to have three post-placement visits, once a month for three months. Our son is four months old and his adoption is still not finalized. Once it is, we are going to have a "forever day" party with all of our family and friends. We didn't have time before he was born to have a baby shower, and since our family wasn't grown the "normal" way, we are going to celebrate that we are different but we are forever family.

As of right now, our son's birth mother and I text almost daily sending pictures and updates and growing our relationship. I also text her mother a lot. They will forever be a part of Ben and who he is, so I will forever love them and they will forever be a part of our family.

Adoption is not new to our family and community. People are usually very kind, generous, and supportive. But there are always people that don't get it, or maybe are uneducated and close-minded. I feel deeply sad for those people. I've had people say things that hurt me for my son and hurt me for myself as an adoptee.

I had people tell me they don't see how you could ever have "your own children" after adopting, that "you could never love them the same," or that "you have to have the experience of pregnancy and birth to have a connection with your child." Also, when people mention "that adoptees have extreme trauma and are likely to commit suicide." I had a person come up to us while we were at dinner and say, "Thank God you didn't adopt a black child."

Other terms and phrases I dislike:

"Paper pregnant." I feel like this takes away from the birth mother's journey and your child's story of who carried him, and makes a joke about it. Seems cheesy, but that's just my opinion.

"So glad you saved him." The Lord is the only one that saves. Our son has changed our lives for the better. We are

not saviors. We didn't adopt for a gold star or to be "good people."

"Now that you've adopted, you're going to get pregnant! I just know it!" We didn't adopt to get pregnant. Adoption is not a good deed that leads to having "your own children."

Questions I get asked are:

- •"Where is he from?"
- •"Was his birth mom on drugs?"
- •"Why didn't his birth mother want him?"
- •"How much was he?"

The list goes on and on. I kindly try and educate people, and pray for them, and for our family.

To adoptees and birth parents: together ALL of us are family, we all are in this together. We are going to make mistakes, but we can grow, educate, learn, and show grace and forgiveness. The most important thing is truly love, to put each other first and love as deep as we can.

Before adopting, I knew God was real. But seeing His plan for our family unfold, the way He brought us to our son and his birth family, there is just no denying that He has a plan and a purpose for everything. He brings beauty from ashes. And I am forever grateful and in awe of Him.

LORI

My name is Lori and I am a single female, and I have wanted to foster children since a young age, and in my mid-20s had the means and stability to do so. I did not choose adoption. I became a foster parent with the intentions of fostering, I had no intentions of adoption until the plan for my daughter (who I fostered) turned from family reunification to adoption.

I met my daughter at eight weeks old, and she was adopted at eleven months old. She is now three years old, we celebrate her adoption day, we discuss her growing in someone else's tummy, and as she grows older, we will continue to add details. Until very recently, I was still fostering other children so the idea of foster care/adoption and parental rights are pretty normal concepts to her. She has always "known" to the best of her age.

To me, adoption is the chance to make a hard situation better for the growth of a child. Adoption is equal parts joyful and heartbreaking.

Best thing said to me about adoption: "Thank you for showing God's love."

Worst thing said to me about adoption: "You have a child DCS (Department of Child Safety) stole."

Adoption is the chance to make a hard situation better for the growth of a child.

I want people to know that adoption is extremely humbling. I also had concerns about adopting a child as a single adult with the future impact on my daughter and any partner. I feel like I'm learning to be a parent on the job (as most do) with the added twist of parenting a child I met and did not birth.

Her name was completely changed at adoption, and at the time, it was important to me that we could sing her name at her first birthday party. Most people look to adopt infants or young children but since I was fostering, it was just how things played out.

I have no relationship with my child's birth parents. None. I do try to follow them on social media, but none seem to be in a place to have healthy relationships with a small child. From my understanding, my daughter is the fifth generation to have contact with DCS/foster care on her maternal side. I look forward to her being the first to live differently.

For the most part, she physically appears to genetically be my child, so I think I am asked a lot less questions by strangers. But most people ask when I will have biological children.

I love these phrases, and I used these phrases all the time when talking about her story:

"Not flesh of my flesh nor bone of my bone but still miraculously my own." I used this quote on her adoption announcement.

"The entire universe conspired to bring me you."

I want people to understand that I did not save her, and I did not do more than most people could. In fact, the best part of my adoption story is my daughter and her fight for life. Adoption is not just for people who cannot have children; adoption is a society and community need we should all feel called to support.

MADELINE

My husband Timothy and I were married in our thirties. After a couple of unsuccessful pregnancies and more unsuccessful infertility surgeries and treatments, we decided to adopt. Timothy is a self-employed CPA, and at the time I worked for a trade association as an office manager. I chose to be a stay-at-home mom after adopting our first child.

We had friends who were adopting domestically and internationally from Russia. After watching their experiences, we decided to pursue adopting from Russia. Primarily, this was due to my incredible fear of adopting domestically and having the birth parents change their minds. I did not think I could handle bonding with a child and then losing them.

Our friends had recently adopted from Siberia and they told us how many children were in orphanages there, approximately half a million back in 1998-99, and as long as we could afford it, it was the better way to go. In 1999, the cost was approximately $30,000.

As a child, I always thought I'd have biological children and then adopt a couple. While I was sad to not be able to have biological children, I never felt like our family was less-than. Adopting our children was the very best blessing, allowing me to be a mom.

We've adopted two children, one internationally and one domestically. Our first, Avery, was adopted from a Russian orphanage in St. Petersburg. She was twenty months old at the time of her adoption, although she'd been in an orphanage since birth. We had very little information about her. The adoption agency (out of Missouri, run by two Russian doctors) sent us a four-minute video and about a paragraph of information. Based upon that, we had to make a lifetime decision.

We had previously declined to adopt a set of twins they'd matched us with. It was heartbreaking to say no, but it was obvious one of the twins was in incredibly poor health. Our friends, who had recently adopted from Siberia, told us to hold out and not take the first kids offered to us since there were thousands of healthy ones. It was very, very hard to say no, but we did *because we could not offer the best for them.*

When they sent us the small amount of info for our daughter, we were given twenty-four hours to decide. We said yes easily due to the fact she seemed healthy on the video and showed annoyance and some emotion. Since I had been busy getting the paperwork and INS (Immigration and Naturalization Service) stuff completed way ahead of time, our adoption experience from signing with the agency until traveling to Russia was only about nine months. It was a long four-month wait after we decided to adopt her before we were given permission to travel.

We had very little info about Avery's size, so we brought several sizes of shoes and clothing, snacks for her, and very little for ourselves. Since Russia is such a gift-giving culture, a large portion of our luggage was dedicated to gifts for the orphanage workers and the adoption team living in Russia. It was surreal!

We were only in Russia five days. At that time, it was a quick turnaround. We were escorted to do paperwork right after landing, then to the orphanage the following day where we got our daughter - after celebrating with the orphanage director with vodka shots. Another surreal experience.

We finalized the adoption in Russian court the following day, then an overnight train to Moscow and the US Embassy. Traveling home from Moscow took twenty-eight hours, including layovers in Germany and Detroit.

This adoption, like most Russian adoptions, was closed except for the fact we received the birthmother's name. This proved beneficial a few years later when we wanted to track her down.

Our second adoption was domestic. We found out through a friend about an adoption agency in Utah that specialized in placing African-American and biracial kids. We had only had Avery for about seven months prior to taking custody of Joshua. He was five days old, born in Las Vegas, Nevada. This was supposed to be semi-open, with both parties having first names only and exchanging pictures and letters every six months.

The agency in Las Vegas mistakenly failed to redact the birth parents' info, so I always had it. Joshua was ill from a very early age. His birth parents had been drug abusers. Birth mother had four prior pregnancies, only one of which she raised herself.

Joshua had health issues that included a hole in his heart, large kidneys, e-coli infection at four months, and some significant learning delays that he continues to deal with today. He was behind, sometimes very far behind, age-appropriate milestones.

Although this adoption was fairly closed, I reached out to the birth mom about five years ago and we have had a good relationship since. We have no relationship with Joshua's birth father as we understand he is still a drug abuser.

We approached telling out children their adoption story by never wanting to hide it, so we decided to annually celebrate "Gotcha Day." I love celebrating "Gotcha Day." As a family, we always celebrated the date of our child coming into our family. For Avery, we chose the date of formal adoption in Russia. For Joshua, we chose the date we took custody since finalizing his domestic adoption ended up taking eleven months. In many ways, it was more important than birthdays because it was just about our family and the treasured moment they became ours and we became theirs.

I don't think there was any special approach. We had lots of bedtime books about adoption and it was a part of natural conversation. We treated adoption as a positive blessing.

This means the kids knew they were adopted from the very beginning. There was never any certain discussion, just a celebration. We never withheld much info on their adoption stories (holding back the bad stuff, of course, until it was age-appropriate), always sharing the blessing of having a birth mom who loved them enough to give them life and make sure they had a good home, and a mom and dad who chose them to be part of our family.

Looking back, I don't think we would change anything. I believe hiding adoption is a huge mistake. After all, to me, adoption is a wonderful earthly example of God's adoption of us (Ephesians 1:5).

By far, most people are kind and supportive. Over the years, people have commended us for being "generous, giving, selfless, brave," and so on. I've always countered that with the fact that we *wanted* children, selfishly, and proceeded to work hard to adopt in order to build our family. Adopting our children wasn't a purely altruistic pursuit.

The worst things said to me came from a Christian woman, whom I've loved and respected for decades, who is also an adoptive mom. She made a comment that upon researching, she believed adoption wasn't really God's plan. It seriously threw me, and I couldn't wrap my brain around her belief. I believe it must come from utter disappointment in her adopted son and his life choices that most definitely don't align with her. Weirdly, that hurt more than passing comments.

I've often had people ask why we had to adopt, what their mother looks like, and some very personal questions. Thankfully, I'd read a good

Adopting our children wasn't a purely altruistic pursuit.

book early in the process that advised adoptive parents to think of the worst comments and prepare calm answers for them. The thinking behind this was that our kids will react and behave as they observe us reacting and behaving. So, prepare your responses as you want your children to respond to questions that seem callous and rude.

One time, when my kids were very little, I was walking with them in a mall. I had my daughter, who is Caucasian, my son who is biracial, and my friend's darker-skinned African-American son. All were under four. A lady who passed me said to her companion, quite loudly, *"Oh look, she's done it with one of every color."* Utterly deplorable, but I ignored it since I had three young ones to tend to. I still can't believe someone would be so obnoxious, but not much surprises me anymore.

I had a grandfather who questioned us adopting a biracial child, as if we couldn't find a white one. He had proudly displayed pictures of our Caucasian daughter but not our son. He often made insensitive, racist remarks. He passed away prior to my kids really remembering him, and they don't know about his attitudes.

I want people to know that adoption has been, primarily, a blessing in our family. It afforded us the opportunity to realize our dreams of raising a family. Our daughter has presented enormous challenges to our family. Not knowing her familial or birth history was concerning, but it didn't deter us from adopting her and giving her a good life.

Our daughter's adoption finalization happened while we were in Russia, at age twenty months. We knew that going in. I wish, with everything I know now, that we would have been able to adopt her when she was much younger. She has significant mental health issues. I truly believe that if she'd had a bonding experience much earlier, some of these problems might have been lessened or averted. We are not currently in any form of positive relationship with her.

Conversely, we adopted our son at birth. Although he has had learning challenges, we believe that having him in our family since birth has given him stability and most importantly, normal attachment. While we took custody of our son at five days old, his adoption wasn't finalized until eleven months. The primary reason for this was that we lived in Arizona, he was born in Nevada, and the adoption agency was in Utah. Basically, it was a tristate procedure and the agency wasn't adept at details with other states. We ended up hiring a great attorney who hashed it all out. I know adopting him from infancy allowed him to fully bond with us.

While I know that adopting older children is a much-needed aspect of adoption, I hope that prospective adoptive parents walk into this process with their eyes wide open. I've often spoken with other adoptive parents about this subject. By and large, we all agree that we went into adoption believing we'd done the research and knew what we were doing. We also STRONGLY believed in Nurture over Nature, yet with years of experience, we now know that we were unprepared and that while nurture *is* extremely important, nature dominates, no matter how well our children were nurtured.

Through an international search organization, we successfully found Avery's birth mother in Russia. The search took over two years and Avery was eleven when we made contact. Birth mother allowed our searcher to interview her on film. We have copies of that as well as her written statement and pictures.

Since she never told her family about having Avery and leaving her in an orphanage, the relationship is informational at best. She and I are friends on social media, and my daughter is friends with her as well. We have not met in person, but we've spoken on the phone once through an interpreter and online a couple of times through an online interpreter.

We had identifying information on our son Joshua's birth parents. Although we'd stopped the biannual letters and pictures when Joshua was six, I reached out to the birth mother through social media about five years ago. A few months after that initial contact, we planned to meet her and her family in Salt Lake City, an approximate halfway point between us in Arizona and her in Montana. Because they were running late, Joshua ended up meeting his mom, for real, at a Wiz Khalifa concert! It was odd, but it took the pressure off of him to make conversation. The rest of the weekend included two days at amusement parks and a couple of dinners.

Joshua is now nineteen years old. Although he doesn't seem too interested in building relationships with his birth mother and half-siblings yet, he is in contact. I am social media friends with her and three of the half-siblings, two of which were also adopted. Birth mother will be joining us in Arizona for Joshua's high school graduation in May and we will be attending the wedding for one of the sisters in Montana this July.

We have always felt that knowledge is important and we never wanted our kids to wonder where they came from. It's human nature to want to know your past and see yourself in others. Within reason, we want to be open with our kids and help them navigate these familial relationships, within the safety of our covering. We never want them to feel guilty about wanting that relationship.

With Avery, it was amazing the way it all came together, how we knew beyond any doubt that she was meant to be our daughter. Even though the last few years have been absolute hell, we have never regretted adopting her, loving her, raising her as our own. Her childhood has given us so many cherished memories.

With our son, we are so thankful for him and the person he is. Although he has significant learning differences, we have always felt incredibly blessed to be the parents who've raised him.

We always get asked the following questions:

- How old were the kids when we adopted them?
- How much did the adoption cost?
- What do their "real parents" look like?
- Are we in contact with birth parents?

I hate when people ask about their "real" parents. *Real parents* are the people that take care of every issue in your young life. I prefer the terms "bio-parents" or "birth parents."

To adoptees I would say this: You are loved, so much, by the parents who raised you. They have struggled, much more than you might realize, to build a family. They didn't go into adoption for praise and accolades, but please try to treat them with respect and kindness, even if you feel like you don't quite fit. If you can, include them in your searches for birth families. Please don't use the fact that you're adopted as a weapon against your parents.

To birth parents, I would say this: Thank you. Thank you for having your child, giving them life when it might seem easier to abort. Thank you for recognizing your inability to properly care for them and sacrificing your desires in favor of their safety, security, and happiness. Please make plans to somehow be a part of your child's history. Write letters to him/her, give photos, leave contact information. This child will someday want information about you, possibly want to know you, and it will positively impact that child's life to have as much information and relationship as possible.

MICHELE

My name is Michele. I'm a graphic designer, my husband works in the software industry, and our son is two years old. We love life and have been blessed abundantly with dear friends and family, travel opportunities, and a church body that has walked with and supported us through all of life's ups and downs.

Whenever I hear stories of people who have wanted to adopt since they were young, I can't help but feel a little bit jealous and sometimes even guilty. My husband and I had no intention of adopting. We always considered it to be a beautiful example of God's grace, redemption, and care, but we were convinced that we weren't called to that life.

We had even had conversations early in our marriage about what we would do if we weren't able to have biological children. The plan was to travel, explore, have fun, and to use our freedom to invest in our friends, family, and church. We honestly never thought we would have to face that reality.

It turns out that my husband and I both deal with infertility issues on some level. We might be able to get pregnant someday but it is highly unlikely. By the time we had figured this out, I was completely broken. God used infertility to show me that the idea of traveling and going on adventures sounded great in theory, but I desperately longed for the cliché pitter-patter of little feet filling my home. Thankfully, it didn't take long for my husband to get on the same page and we dove right in without any hesitation or second-guessing.

Our adoption was a domestic, transracial, infant adoption. I was at a friend's house having coffee when our agency called me to let me know that we had been chosen. "You were chosen by a beautiful mother and she gave birth to a perfect baby boy two days ago." It was a complete and total shock. We thought we were going to have a month or more to prepare, but instead, we would be able to meet him in a week and a half.

I rushed home as fast as I could to tell my husband the incredible news. There was a truck in front of me on the road who was driving at what felt like a snail's pace. I'm absolutely positive that God put him there to stop me from getting into a car wreck. We also had airline vouchers that were going to expire a week later so we didn't have to worry about the cost of our plane tickets.

After we picked him up, we had a beautiful home all to ourselves to stay in while we waited on the appropriate paperwork to go through so that we could travel back to our home state. My mom was even able to be with us when we traveled because the timing was perfectly aligned with her work schedule. I could list out so many other details that blew us away and I'm sure that God took care of countless other things that we didn't even notice. He has everything under control and I'm so thankful that I can count on Him to take care of it all.

After we had our son in our care for about a week, we were able to meet his birth parents. We were so grateful that they were willing to connect with us in this way. On our way to meet them, I was so incredibly nervous. I was so scared that we wouldn't be able to connect or that they would regret their choice after meeting us face-to-face.

Once we started talking and I realized how similar we all were, I became much more relaxed. They were so easy to talk to and we fell in love with them instantly. It was really special to be able to ask each other questions and get to know each other a little bit. Watching them say goodbye to our son was one of the hardest things I have ever experienced. It was gut-wrenching and I still get choked up whenever I think about that moment.

Our relationship with them is now semi-open. We send pictures, letters, and updates to our agency and they pass it along. All communication goes through the agency. Our son's birth parents can send things back to us if they'd like but they haven't yet. We are very hopeful that they will someday want a fully open adoption with us.

We haven't really had to worry about telling our son about his adoption story yet since he's still so young. We plan on keeping adoption an open topic of conversation and simply answer questions as they come. When we met with his birth parents, they allowed us to take a photo with them and we have that framed in his room. Our hope is that he always understands who they are and what they sacrificed for him. We have kept many details of their life to ourselves in an effort to ensure that he hears about those things directly from us when he's ready.

Finalization can feel like you're finally able to release a breath that you don't even know you're holding.

Adoption is a beautiful gift. I am fully aware that it is born from brokenness. There is pain and trauma there that can never fully go away. But for me, as a barren woman, adoption is the most beautiful manifestation of God's love for me. It's the reason my son is mine. In a perfect, sinless, unbroken world, my son's birth parents wouldn't have had to choose someone else to parent their child. He would still be with them and it is unlikely that I would even know him. The

194

fact that he's in my life is a complete miracle and one of the greatest gifts that God has ever given me. I am completely blown away by the magnitude of it and am so thankful that this is the life that God had in store for me.

The worst thing that anyone has said to us was, "I wonder if he would have preferred being raised by a black family instead?" To be fair, this was asked by a woman who was in her mid-nineties and had been dealing with memory loss. I honestly don't think she meant anything malicious at all, she was simply stating out loud a thought that had entered her mind. I try not to worry about it but sometimes it *is* really hard for me to shake. I worry that that's what everyone else is actually thinking when they look at my family. I'm so afraid that they analyze me and my husband and wonder if we'll be able to honor our son's heritage as well as he deserves.

And honestly, my fear is that their concerns are justified. How can this *very* white couple really be able to help him understand where he comes from and prepare him for the struggles he will likely face one day? Will he have major identity struggles that we can't help him navigate? Will he feel isolated and alone? Will he grow to resent us? I really don't know. By the grace of God, he may never struggle with his racial identity, but the idea that we can't relate to such an impactful part of his life is very hard. I can only hope that God gives us wisdom and that He gives our son the ability to forgive us in the areas where we fail.

Most of the things that people say to us are positive. I love when people comment on how alike our son is to us. He and my husband are especially similar and share a very beautiful bond with one another. I love when people focus on that as the special gift that it is for them to be so much alike even though they're not biologically connected. It gives me a sense of belonging with our son that I think is really wonderful and I'm so grateful for it.

Meeting him for the first time at two weeks old meant that he still felt like a newborn for the most part. Knowing him from such a young age is such a gift, but I was disappointed about not being with him straight from the hospital. I was so sad to miss out on those first two weeks of his life.

His foster parents were absolutely incredible, though. They sent me pictures and updates every day and told me all about the little quirks and things they were seeing so that I could feel as involved as possible. I am forever thankful for how well they cared for him and how much love they poured into him even though their time with him was temporary. God took a situation that had originally made me sad and turned it into an opportunity to meet two of the most selfless people. I had the opportunity to witness absolute unconditional love firsthand.

Our son's adoption wasn't finalized in court until he was about nine months old. Once everything was official, a huge weight was lifted from our shoulders. I've heard it said that finalization can feel like you're finally able to release a breath that you don't even know you're holding. I truly didn't realize just how anxious I was about losing him until it all became official.

In general, people are very curious about our son's birth parents. They want to know about our relationship with them and their circumstances that lead them to adoption. It's hard to answer these questions honestly without giving away too many private details that should remain within our family. We don't want our son to find out any intimate details about his origins from someone who doesn't have a right to that information in the first place.

I really don't appreciate when people (especially strangers) praise us for adopting. One of the common things that people will say is that "he is so lucky to be in your family" or "I just think that what you guys have done is amazing." I know that those things come from a good place but I don't like this idea that we saved him or that we're so much better than his birth parents. We are just different. We have been blessed with certain circumstances that they wanted for him. But he may very well have thrived with them. There is no way to know for sure and it is so incredibly unfair to assume. It annoys me when people imply that we're some sort of savior figures. We are simply two people who wanted to be parents.

But I absolutely love it when strangers say things like, "Your son is so adorable," or, "You have a beautiful family." I really don't mind when people want to talk about adoption and if we were to sit down over coffee, I'd be more than happy to spill my heart out about the beauty and pain I've experienced. When it comes to idle chit-chat, however, it feels great when adoption is left out of the conversation entirely. My family is more than adoption.

My hope for adoptees is that their identity would never start and end with the fact that they were adopted. While I understand that that's a large part who they are, it's not *all* that they are. I hope they're able to see themselves through God's eyes, because His opinion of them is the only one that truly matters. I want them to see the big picture that He has for their lives and be able to find true joy in the fact that He chose them and loved them long before anyone applied any sort of label to their lives. His plan for them is as unique as they are and growing up with parents who didn't give birth to them is just one aspect of a beautiful picture that's so much larger than any of us can even fathom.

I hope that birth parents (especially my son's) understand that we adoptive parents are really trying. We may not know how to love or honor them perfectly. We will fail. But we're trying to do the right thing. We want to do the right things for our children, their birth parents, our families, and ourselves. It's a lot to balance, nothing is black and white, and it's hard. Please be gracious and kind to us as we navigate these unknown and challenging waters.

I wish people could understand that even though our adoption story was pretty picture perfect (from an adoptive parent's point of view), it is still hard. Our story is still laced with grief, adoption guilt, depression, and so much fear. It would be really easy to look at the outward details of our story and think that there is no way for it to have turned out better. And that's probably true. We didn't experience the pain of a failed placement, we love his birth family, and we didn't have any issues bonding with him.

But that doesn't mean that it hasn't come with struggles and that we're free from any adoption-related challenges. We must keep in mind moving forward that there is trauma in our son's story that we will never fully understand and it could be tempting to pretend like it's not present at all. On the flip side, we don't want to assume that all bad behaviors stem from adoption-related trauma. It's so hard to know what's going on in your child's heart - and life is never as simple as we'd like it to be.

The best part of our adoption story was how perfectly God executed every last detail. We had to completely let go of any sort of control that we thought we had and let Him take care of it all for us. And He totally delivered.

PENNY

My name is Penny, and I am a stumbling follower of Jesus, learning to love like him, to be loved by him, to tell the truth with grace, and to advocate for those who wonder if they matter. I live in a small town in Maryland with my husband - my greatest adventure yet. Sometimes we bicker but mostly we just laugh at the chaos that is our life.

We parent four kids, two came to us through adoption, one has Down syndrome. Our days are often full of laughter, dancing, tween-age angst, curious tots, hard conversations, and heaps of forgiveness.

I work as a writer to create a sense of belonging in my readers and to inspire them to consider how they love and serve those who are often ignored, excluded, or dismissed by the Church. In the midst of parenting, writing, and maintaining the trifecta of marriage, home, and community, I'm grateful for strong coffee, belly laughs, good books, and long walks.

We chose adoption because we wanted to write a better story for our lives and we knew that would require leaps of faith, discomfort, and surrender. We knew this meant we would play a part in caring for children in need of families.

While I watched my two year-old girl play and snuggled my newborn boy, a man drawled to me, "Yep. Now you've got the million dollar family." That comment bothered me, mainly because we had never made that our goal. A few years after this comment, my husband and I began to sense a divine nudge toward adoption.

In our prayers and conversations behind closed doors, we began to ask questions like, "What kind of life are we creating? What else might God be calling us to? Where is the world hurting and what is our role in it?"

As we wrestled through our answers, we were led to vulnerable children, the ones harder to place, those with disabilities. That led us to adopting a child with Down syndrome. Eighteen months later, we brought our newborn son home.

In the spring of 2016, we began to consider adoption again. Two months later, we heard from an acquaintance in a complicated situation. She wondered if we'd be willing to adopt her baby. In early 2017, we brought our newborn daughter home.

Both children were three-to-six months old when we adopted them. Making their adoptions legal at such young ages was expected, according to the protocol of each state's court. Finalization felt like an official seal, an external confirmation that the necessary requirements had been met for us to legally parent these dear ones.

I had no prior relationship with my son's birth relatives. I met his birth mom the day before his birth and his birth dad and other relatives on the day of his birth. They are such lovely, caring people and we have a healthy, open relationship with frequent contact via text or email and social media.

I had vaguely known my daughter's birth mom for a few years before I moved out of state, then reconnected with her on social media a few years later. Initially, I believe her profound grief, inadequate post-placement support, and poor counseling led to unhealthy patterns in her obsessive contact. Her guilt and pain nearly swallowed me. In our efforts to create a sustainable future relationship, we worked with our agency to create healthy boundaries that gave us the necessary time to bond and allowed our daughter's birth mom to begin to heal.

With time, good therapy, and prayer, we have grown to be good friends, maintaining a vibrant open relationship in which we communicate through hilarious GIFs, texts, and social media. We care about each other as fellow humans and mothers and we both want the best for the daughter who brought our families together.

With their current developmental stages (ages four and two), I briefly but consistently share their stories, sparing unnecessary details for now. Into their young ears, I speak of their brave birth moms having to make a hard choice. I assure them they were moved from one pair of loving arms to another. Telling their stories now helps me to find appropriate language that I adapt as they grow.

Adoption is a lifelong willingness to embrace a sacred paradox. It is a complicated blend of profound loss and tremendous gain, of unspeakable joy and crushing grief, of selfless surrender and deliberate decisions, of anguished cries and answered prayers, of wondering whether or where we belong and discovering we always belonged, of hidden wounds and radical healing, of absolute terror and divine courage, of opening our hearts and guarding our hearts, of total devastation and the promise of hope in the wreckage.

Adoption is an invitation for me to enter the stories of my children's first families, to bear witness to their pain, to graciously accept their request to do what they wish they could. Adoption is an invitation to walk with my children through their stories, to give them space to connect with their first families, to equip them now as I help them navigate the road ahead.

Adoption is a lifelong willingness to embrace a sacred paradox.

Worst comments I've received:
- "Why didn't her mom want her?"

- "Why would you adopt a Mongoloid?"
- "You guys are amazing." (Insert gagging noise.)

Likewise, I get asked:
- "Why'd their moms give them up?"
- "Are they your real kids?"
- "How much does adoption cost?"
- "Where are they from?"

Also, I hate hearing people say:
- "I'd adopt but I can't afford to."
- "I could never do that."
- "I'd adopt but my husband doesn't want to."
- "Gave up for adoption."

Best comments:
- "Adoption will break your heart in the best kind of way."
- "Your family is beautiful - so diverse! Keep loving each other like Jesus."

And I always love to hear:
- "Parenting is hard. You're doing a fantastic job!"
- "Her hair looks so good - you're doing a great job with it." (As a transracial adoptive mom learning to style biracial hair, this means the world to me, es-

pecially when I hear it from my black and brown friends.)

What do I want others to know about my adoptive parent experience? First, that I owe you nothing about the details of my children's stories. They are not mine to tell. Second, that I need you to care and support us long after the baby showers and initial cuteness wears off and we settle into the reality of loss and trauma and a new family structure. Adoption is worth every tumultuous moment because children and birth families are worthy to be seen and loved.

I wish people could understand that adoption is not binary. It is not a competitive relationship with birth families. While I am the mother raising them, I am not their only mother and that must be acknowledged, accepted, and embraced. As an adoptive mom, I am invited to create space for a growing, collaborative relationship with my kiddos' birth families, where the love of Christ abounds in all our imperfections, and his grace holds us through every season.

The best part of it all has been discovering that my capacity to love my children is far greater than I imagined and that my empathy for their birth families seems to strengthen with time. Surely, this a divine work in me.

Adoptees and birth parents: By the grace of God, I'll do my best to listen to your pain, to inform my corner of the world of your vital roles, to turn the spotlight away from me so you can be seen, to pass the mic so your voices can be amplified, to educate myself on the issues that impact our families, to maintain my own emotional health to better serve you, and to love you in ways that feel meaningful to you.

We could have made different choices. We could have said "yes" to the stereotypical million dollar family. We could have said "no" to different abilities, to birth families in crisis. We could have decreased the drama, shut out the heartache, and opted for a less complicated life. But we would have missed the depth and richness that adoption has brought to our lives - the ways we have been shattered and are slowly being rebuilt as a result of our family dynamic.

SHANNON

My name is Shannon and I am the mother of two adult adopted daughters ages thirty-seven and twenty-nine. Both of them have rewarding careers and are following their dreams. They are very close to one another and have a loving relationship with me and their dad. Both of them have mild to moderate anxiety disorders.

Between my husband's low sperm count and my history of anovulation, I had a difficult time getting and staying pregnant. We had a close family friend who was a supervisor for foster care for our county's Department of Human Services and encouraged us to apply for adoption. We adopted our first child this way. It took about a year and it was a grueling experience. We filled out endless paperwork, had several home visits, and attended mandatory parenting classes. Throughout the entire process, the red tape from the first interview to the moment that Bree, my eight-week old baby girl, was in my arms, it seemed painfully endless.

Our youngest daughter was adopted privately through an attorney, because at that time, Human Services had a policy, due to their long waiting list, that a family could only adopt once. It took six years of "self-marketing" my desire to adopt again - and talking to anyone who would listen - to finally get a second opportunity. My OB/GYN had a patient that wanted to place her newborn in an adoptive home. Jane was four days old when she became our newest family member.

Both adoptions were local and closed but human error gave me the birth mother's name of both girls. Bree was a preemie and needed supplements. The birth mother was listed on the label of the baby vitamins from the hospital that were given to us by the agency. Jane's birth mother was revealed when the attorney's secretary accidentally sent us hospital records that listed the birth mother. I think these types of accidents were meant to be and aren't really accidents. That information became important and useful as their lives unfolded.

Bree and Jane were told about their adoption at a very early age - around two years old. We wanted them to never remember a time where they didn't know their history. We started off with a very simple but true version of their adoption, usually after a bedtime story.

Something like, "Mommy and Daddy tried and tried to make a baby grow inside mommy's tummy, but weren't able to make that happen. We were very sad. So we spoke to a nice lady that helped us make a family through adoption. We waited and waited and waited. One wonderful day, this nice lady called us to tell us that our perfect baby girl had finally arrived. That was the happiest day of our lives!" This was always followed up with some big hugs and kisses.

As they aged, the story became more complex, trying to answer their questions as honestly as we were able. When the question "Why was I put up for adoption?" was asked, I told them that the woman who gave birth to her loved her and wanted her to have the type of family that she wasn't able to provide. Never, never did I ever say anything negative about their birth parents or give any unnecessary details I might have known that would have caused my daughters lasting pain or shake their perception of self-worth. If no good could come from it, I spared them the anguish.

I wouldn't change anything about the way this was executed. My daughters have always known and felt that they were wanted, chosen and unconditionally loved. When they were each around thirteen, they asked about finding their birth mothers. I told them that when they reached eighteen, I would help them in their search if they were agreeable to receive counseling through the search process. I told them that they would most likely find one of three scenarios:

1. You find someone that welcomes you into their life. You can't have too many people in this world that love you.
2. Meeting you could remind them of a very difficult time in their life and they could reject you. This could be very hurtful.
3. This person sees the advantages you have been blessed with and feels you owe them something.

This seemed to resonate as neither of them expressed a desire to find their birth parents after they turned eighteen.

Intelligent people with little or no connection to adoption can sound really foolish sometimes. I remember my old college roommate telling me that we didn't need to adopt. According to her, all we need to do is drink a couple of beers at a drive-in movie, hop in the backseat, and *boom*, I would be pregnant!

The best thing ever said about adoption came from my mom. Someone asked her which one of her grandchildren were adopted. Her response: "I forget."

A funny story: At fourteen, Bree's adopted friend Amanda said she was going to go on *Oprah* when she was eighteen to find her birth mother. She was sure it was Mariah Carey. Bree's retort was, "What do you need more parents for? Don't you have enough parents telling you what to do?"

Although I do not have a relationship with any of the four birth parents, both of my daughters have one birth parent that have located and contacted them. Local adoption in a small midwestern community carries that risk. Neither of my daughters have chosen to have any ongoing communication with their known birth parents.

This sad situation rests solely on the birth parents and how they reacted. They were pushy. They tried to force a relationship. They stalked our daughters on social media or sent them countless emails. They insisted that they were to be called "mom" or "dad," regardless of my daughters' feelings about doing so. They showed up unexpectedly in public places where they knew the girls would be and confronted them. They immediately wanted their birth daughters to meet all of their relatives. Wrong on so many levels!

I know both my daughters had some pretty bizarre encounters with their respective birth parents but that is their story to tell. I did, however, contact Bree's birth mom when she turned twenty-one to tell her that our daughter was a healthy, bright woman about to graduate from college with honors. She was grateful for the call and said her husband and children were aware of the adoption, and she would not contact Bree out of respect for her and us. But if Bree needed any genetic counseling, she would be happy to contribute. I passed along her contact information to Bree. I'm not sure what she did with it.

For the first time in close to a decade, one of my daughters and I are having in-depth discussions about adoption, and how it is affecting her adult psyche. Long overdue! It took a rare argument, where in a heated moment Bree blurted out that she was "given away" at birth, to rekindle this conversation. We both began to read *Through Adopted Eyes* and are using many of the memoirs as a vehicle to facilitate these heartfelt talks. This exchange, as difficult and even painful as it can sometimes be for both of us, is leading her to a deeper understanding of herself. Self-love is the key to the things she holds dear - maintaining healthy and happy relationships with her husband and my bright and talented twelve-year-old grandson.

The comment I hate the most is, "Oh, you had a baby the easy way."

I don't get asked adoption questions very often. When I do, I try to answer as simply and honestly as I can. The comment I hate the most is, "Oh, you had a baby the easy way." My response is always the same, "No, YOU had a baby the easy way. I had to jump through a thousand hoops to make my family."

The thing that I would like others to know about a family knitted together by adoption is that it is little to no different than a traditional family. As a parent, I really never thought of my girls as adopted. They were my girls with no strings attached. The only obvious difference is in their physical appearance and the uncertainty of where their innate skills and talents come from. It was fun to explore music and art lessons, academic competitions, and sports to find out. Also, an adoptive parent doesn't automatically attribute negative personality traits from other family members: "You're stubborn, just like your Uncle Mike!"

Adoption has been the single most defining event of my life's story. It has shaped who I am and created my beautiful family. It has made my life a blessing. Not that it has been easy. There were plenty of arguments, lots of hysteria and door slamming along the journey. At times, I thought that screaming had become my normal tone of voice.

Who knows what might have been if I had given birth to two children rather than adopted them? There are plenty of genetic issues in both mine and my ex-husband's heredity to have warranted a turbulent household. Based on my brothers' and friends' family experiences, mine wasn't a whole lot different. I think that this is the biggest takeaway for those curious about adoption: Once that child becomes YOUR child, your life unfolds pretty much like every other family.

If adoptees and birth parents read between the lines of my story, they will see everything I want them to know, along with any pearls of wisdom I have to offer. Every family dynamic is unique, but when it comes to raising children - adopted or not - love, tolerance, compassion, consistency, and setting the standard by example are always a good start.

BUILDING HEARTS

It may seem like an obvious statement to make that adoption connects people, but it does so in more ways than one may think. If there is one thing I hope you can take away from these stories, it is for you to realize how important it is to help support all of the members of the adoption triad. But don't just realize it - go out there and *do* it!

Adoption agencies should speak realistically and truthfully about the adoption process to their prospective clients and more post-adoption services need to be made available for the *whole* triad. It is exciting that people are really starting to talk about adoption rather than sweep it under the rug, but there is still more we can do.

If you are a member of the triad, I would encourage you to flip back to pages 17-19 and answer the questions for yourself that the book participants answered. No matter if you are connected to adoption or not, writing has a therapeutic effect. Reach out and support members of your community. Write your thoughts down and create a book like I did. Maybe you don't publish it with the whole world, but consider the powerful impact you can make in someone's life!

I am not kidding – you should really write down your thoughts! Go for it! Doodle on this next page. Get some ideas down on paper. I will not be mad if you mark in this book. Keep writing and sharing. Who knows?

Besides writing, I really enjoy going on walks. When I am walking, I have noticed that there are a lot of shapes in nature. Leaves and flowers often have three points. Many bridges do, too. The triangle is supposed to be the strongest shape, right? Yet it seems that the lines that make up the triangle of the adoption triad are feeble and easily blown away. Distrust, misinformation, stereotypes, and brokenness hurt each side of the adoption triad, weakening what should be strong.

However, instead of focusing on each side's disunity, let us first look at what makes a triangle…a triangle. No one triad is perfect and there is not only one kind of triangle. Triangles can have different heights, each side can be a different length. The thing that makes a triangle a triangle is this: it has three sides supporting each other. A triangle is unique in its naturally supportive structure.

I hope this book strengthens the triad. Some triad members may feel that love is missing from their triangle or their triangle is incomplete. Some may not want to think about their triad triangle. But, instead of viewing each side as being torn away from each other, I want to think about how we can strengthen our triangles. We can use *hearts* to strengthen them. Let me show you!

Picture a heart shape in your mind - now put it inside of the triangle that represents your triad. The heart supports the sides of the triangle - so even the most wobbly, incomplete structure can hold steady with the help of some heart.

Adoptees have to learn how to love the idea of (and accept the reality of) both sets of parents and the part each plays in their lives. As hard as that may be for some, both sets of parents are part of that individual's journey - there's no escape from that. I know, I know...easier said than done, but accepting this is key to healing.

Likewise, birth parents need to learn to love the adoptive parents caring for their children with the same love they have for their children who were placed. Likewise, adoptive parents need to be able to love their child's birth family, even though the circumstances were very difficult, as an extension of their love for their child.

Love is what makes the triad stronger. Adoption has many factors, but realizing where the love is can make healing a lot less painful.

You may draw out your own triad. Maybe you think it looks incomplete and unstable. Maybe, like me, you have missing edges, creating partial shapes. Even if we may never fully reconstruct our specific triangle, we should not be afraid to allow other triad members to help us strengthen and build back up our side of the triad and help them in their journeys as well.

Build up others with encouraging words, point them to resources you've found helpful, and be there for each other even before someone cries out for help. Redefine what your triangle looks like by finding adoption buddies that can help represent their triad space well. If we allow ourselves to learn from each side, then together we can each build back our triangle through adopted hearts.

STORY INDEX

Due to the breadth and scope of different stories represented in this book, we wanted to provide readers with an index to help them quickly return to stories representative of various popular topics concerning adoption.

ADOPTIVE PARENTS, OPEN ADOPTIONS

ALLISON   CHARLOTTE & MASON
ELIZABETH   JENNIFER
KENDALL   LEIGHA
LENA   LILI
MADELINE   PENNY

ADOPTIVE PARENTS, CLOSED ADOPTIONS

AMELIA   CHRISTA
DANIELLE & FORD   KALEB & DEMI
LEIGHA   LORI
MADELINE   SHANNON

ADOPTIVE PARENTS, DOMESTIC

ALLISON	CHARLOTTE & MASON
ELIZABETH	KENDALL
LILI	MADELINE
MICHELE	PENNY

ADOPTIVE PARENTS, ADOPTED OUT OF FOSTER CARE

BETHANY	JENNIFER
KALEB & DEMI	LEIGHA
LENA	LORI

ADOPTIVE PARENTS, INTERNATIONAL

AMELIA	CHRISTA
DANIELLE & FORD	MADELINE

ADOPTIVE PARENTS, TRANSRACIAL

AMELIA	BETHANY
CHRISTA	ELIZABETH
KALEB & DEMI	MADELINE
PENNY	

ADOPTIVE PARENT AND ADOPTEE
LILI

ADOPTIVE PARENT, SINGLE PARENT
LORI

BIRTH PARENTS, OPEN
ABBIE   APRIL
AUBREY   BROOKLYN
DESIRAE   ERICA
LINDIE   MONIQUA
REAGAN   SARAH

BIRTH PARENTS, SEMI-OPEN
CAMILA   KELSEY
NORA   SAMANTHA
SKYLAR   TIA

RECOMMENDED RESOURCES

While we hope that this book is a treasured resource for you, we also recommend you check out the following resources concerning adoption and related topics:

Books
- *The Connected Child: Bring Hope and Healing To Your Adoptive Family* by Karyn Purvis
- *The Body Keeps the Score: Brain, Mind, and Body in the Healing of Trauma* by Bessel van der Kolk M.D.

Online/Other
- Ashley Mitchell/Lifetime Healing LLC - lifetimehealingadoption.com
- Adopt Well - www.adoptwell.com
- Christa Jordan - spoonfulofjordan.com
- Kate Carper - katecarper.com
- Cameron Lee Small/Therapy Redeemed - therapyredeemed.wordpress.com
- Brett and Dave-O/Yes I'm Adopted: Don't Make It Weird - yesimadopted.com

- Wreckage & Wonder - <u>wreckageandwonder.com/blog</u>
- Adoption Keys - @adoptioneducationkeys

Also, feel free to follow @ThroughAdoptedEyes on Instagram to see who I am connecting with!

ABOUT THE AUTHOR

Elena S. Hall holds a Master of Social Work from the University of Texas at Arlington and her passion for adoption advocacy stems from her faith and family. She loves to write, dance, sing, and tell stories. Her goal is to aid those in the adoption triad to promote healing and growth within the adoption community and empower readers to share their own stories.

Made in the USA
Monee, IL
05 October 2022

15276670R00142